CLARET PRESS

Book design: Petya Tsankova
Illustration on back cover: Weimin He

ISBN paperback: 978-1-910461-58-7
ISBN ebook: 978-1-910461-59-4

A CIP catalogue record for this book is available from the British Library.

This paperback can be ordered from all bookstores as well as from Amazon, and the ebook is available on online platforms such as Amazon and iBooks.

www.claretpress.com

FOOD of LOVE

cooking up a life across gender, class and race

Sylvia Vetta

Sylvia Vetta

There are only four questions of importance in life.

What is sacred, what the spirit is made of,
what is worth living for, and what is worth dying for.

The answer to all of them is the same.

ONLY LOVE.

Umberto Eco

CONTENTS

APPETISER

I was born on a cold grey day in December 1945 in Luton, in a house like everyone else's in the district: without central heating and where hot water was so precious that the immersion heater was switched on for only two hours a day. The men had just come back from the war and the women left their jobs to devote themselves to home, husband and children. Everyone in the street was white.

My working-class childhood was three changes of clothes, a few toys and privilege. I was English and therefore had inherited the earth. On Empire Day, my teacher, Mr Watson, pinned a map to the blackboard and pointed out that two thirds of the earth was coloured pink. *'The most extensive empire the world had ever seen,'* he said as he moved his stick to a small island off the northern coast of Europe, *'is ruled from here.'* We were taught Kipling's view of the world: *East is east and west is west and never the twain shall meet.*

That was about to change. Post World War 2 new immigrants from all corners of the globe explained their presence: *We're here because you were there.*

Britain was about to go through one of its rare transformations, a root-and-branch reform of its core elements: race, sex, creed, class, economic organisation, social make-up. Profound and rapid change affected me, like my entire generation. My story is of chance encounters with good people and misogynists, with visionaries and racists, in a time of a quiet metamorphosis. It has been extraordinary—if occasionally exhausting—to have been part of that.

Food is one of humanity's ways of expressing love. Most cultures express love through sustaining life with nourishment enhanced with pleasure. Food will flow through my narrative like the great rivers of the world that connect us. I love to cook for those I love, and I deeply appreciate the meals that have been lovingly made for me. The British diet I grew up with was stodgy, stolid and predictable. Who from my parent's generation could have predicted that curry would become my country's favourite dish?

My older brother Ray adored travel but was reluctant to sample local food, whereas for my other brother, Mike, and for me it is one of the greatest pleasures of exploration. Food has become an aspect of diversity that both left and right relish: it holds no prejudice-inducing fear. The recipes at the end of chapters reflect the diversity in our diet that has arisen from our growing diversity. People often fear difference but nothing illustrates better the pleasures that come with immigration than the recipes in this book. My mother's English cream tea and my Cornish grandmother's pasties have not gone away but now we can also taste the world.

This cultural enrichment is not only evident in our food but also in music and dance, art and language, gardens and architecture and so much more. It's sad that the hard right has encouraged my fellow Brits to claim that British culture is under threat from change, instead of recognising our culture's resilience and its capacity to expand and encompass.

Three miles from where I live is a house with a shark in the roof—a symbol that life is not predictable. You need to expect the unexpected. That's perhaps the best advice I can offer.

Aged seven, I discovered libraries and a love of reading and writing but the idea that a working-class girl from Luton could become an author was as crazy as eating the straw boater with which my birth-place was associated. My parents had saved to buy us a set of Arthur Mee's children's encyclopaedias, and those books and the local museum I biked to fostered a love of history in me. If you had told the ten-year-old me that I'd become the director of an art and antiques centre, I'd have had to search in those encyclopaedias to find out what on earth you were talking about.

When I interviewed Chris Patten, the Chancellor of Oxford University, I asked him, '*What would he, when a student at Oxford, have said if told he'd one day become the Chancellor?*' He shrugged and said that he would've suggested the speaker was high on marijuana!

If middle-class Lord Patten of Barnes's future was so unexpected, how much more so was mine? Women were second-class citizens and working-class women were at the bottom of the pile. So my story inevitably shows the intersection of that class, that race and that gender at one point in history. There is a specificity to my changes, although I share them with many women walking in the same shoes. I hope my story offers some insight into what it was like to be acted on by those forces of history and to be a small part of embracing and building on those changes.

Mum and Dad's wedding 21 December 1928

Expect the unexpected: The Headington Shark created by John Buckley.

CHAPTER 1: Flopsy 1952

When Flopsy was served up in a stew, I couldn't eat her. I'd fed my rabbit groundsel from the waste land at the bottom of Pomfret Avenue and bolted lettuce from my father's allotment. Dad had no problem doing the necessaries. His father and grandfather were butchers with land near Sennen Cove, overlooking Land's End in Cornwall. My reluctance to eat Flopsy pointed the way to becoming a vegetarian in 1987, a concept which I knew nothing about until I met my husband.

Charles Thomas Harry, my father, was born in 1902 in St Buryan, Cornwall and, by the age of two, had lost his own father. His mother, Elizabeth, remarried a year later, and Charles never inherited his father's land or the butcher's shop in St Buryan. Instead his stepfather gave Charles the motorbike in the picture as his inheritance. How he loved that dream machine! That gift determined his life. He trained as an apprentice mechanic with Vauxhall Motors in Vauxhall, London and then joined the RAF. When he was stationed at Henlow Camp, he drove his bike through the village of Stotfold and captured the heart of my mother, Doris Howard. They married in 1928 when she was eighteen and he was twenty six, and in the act, Charles gained a large extended family.

Stotfold 1928: Dad's precious motorbike

Grandma and Grandpa in the centre. Doris is at the front between Charles and Arthur. My favourite Aunt Alice is standing behind my grandmother. For a while all the girls worked at the Spirella corset factory in Letchworth.

On April Fools' Day in 1957, the weekly documentary programme, Panorama, broadcast a three-minute spoof report of the spaghetti harvest in Switzerland, showing attractive young women lifting strings of pasta off bushes. Hundreds phoned the BBC the next day for advice on how to grow their own spaghetti tree. Many more fell for the joke.

The narrow culinary experience of most Brits was a main meal of meat and two boiled veg, with fish on Fridays. My mother was not alone in cooking a roast dinner every Sunday. On Monday—wash day— we ate cold meat, potatoes and salad. On Tuesday, Doris would grind the remaining leftovers and make shepherd's pie. We ate mint sauce with lamb, parsley sauce with fish, horseradish with beef and apple sauce with pork. My mum prepared her own ham and tongue. Every Friday I'd come home from school to a house fragrant with the aroma of baked cakes. I can't remember one spoiled meal.

My mother had grown up on a smallholding in Stotfold, Bedford-shire. When I interviewed Icolyn Smith, the founder of the Cowley Road Soup Kitchen in Oxford, she described how she was born of sub-sistence farmers in Jamaica. Her experience of food sounded so like my mother's. The two-up two-down house accommodating my grand-parents and their nine children would have been more solid than Ico-lyn's, but apart from that, subsistence farming describes it well.

Mum's brother Arthur and his wife Bertha continued to live there after my grandparents died when I was six and seven respectively. I loved visiting. Many of the Howard tribe were in the Salvation Army and played brass instruments but Bertha owned and played on an upright piano. My favourite aunt, Alice, who became an officer in the Salvation Army, was a proficient pianist. (More about her later.) The family liked to gather around the piano and sing hymns and popular songs. At the bottom of the garden was an orchard and beyond that soft fruit. My parents were used to just-picked freshness.

Towards the end of the war they bought the semi-detached house in Luton in which I was born. My dad's peacetime job was as a rectification fitter at the now American-owned, Vauxhall Motors factory. Our house was unusual in being newly built in early 1945. Italian prisoners of war laid the road in Pomfret Avenue. Some of the neighbours criticised my mother when she plied the prisoners with cups of tea. Her brother Horace was a prisoner of war in Germany captured in North Africa and she empathised. My favourite uncle, Charlie, was a sergeant in the Forgotten Army in Burma. When he returned he could find nowhere for his wife Eva and himself to live, so they squatted in a Nissen Hut in the New Forest until in 1949 they moved into a new council house in Petersfield. Charlie loved Eva to bits and all he wanted was to enjoy what he could of life. I never persuaded him to answer questions about Burma and to my knowledge, all he ever said, even to Eva, was that his officer was killed and he had to find a way of getting his men back to India.

Many decades later I had the privilege of interviewing that master of speculative fiction, Brian Aldiss. Sixty years after WW2, I could taste the fear that came from the slightest rustle in the jungle as he described his experience as a soldier in Burma. Private Aldiss, with other veterans of that war in the east, arrived home in Southampton to be met on the docks by NO ONE, not even a representative from the army. Truly the forgotten army.

Father had an allotment half a mile from our house where I learned how to trench potatoes and pick peas, eating a lot raw as I worked. One Saturday afternoon as I walked home alone, I passed a man standing by a narrow alley. It wasn't until I was close to him that he turned around displaying his erect penis. That was the first time I'd seen that particular male organ. I ran home but didn't tell my mother—I didn't have the vocabulary. Sex, biology, reproduction, sexuality were not topics at that time for any child, or indeed most adults. I'm not exaggerating.

Although the vegetables I picked were mostly boiled, they had flavour. It is hard for my grandchildren to grasp the idea of an orange or a satsuma being so precious that it was a star ingredient in my Christmas stocking. My parents were not unusual in post-war Britain buying their first refrigerator in 1958. Before that, food had to be bought fresh and vegetables were only available in season. In the winter, we ate whatever could be conserved: cabbage, cauliflower, sprouts and root veg. Tomatoes, often called 'love apples' because they evoked the colour of ruby red lips, were only available in the summer and early autumn when courting was easy. The first aubergine I saw was a sad-looking shrivelled thing imported by an Asian shopkeeper in Smethwick in 1963. No wonder a diet without meat was unusual.

While at primary school, I came home for lunch but it wasn't called lunch; it was called dinner and was the main meal of the day. The evening meal was 'tea'. The idea of eating out was not just foreign, it was unaffordable. The only meals I experienced before secondary school, apart from my mother's cooking, were take-away fish and chips, meals at aunts and every other year a week's summer holiday in a boarding house. Bill Bryson described it well in *Notes from a Small Island.*

Mrs Smegma... gave me a tour of the facilities and outlined the many complicated rules for residing there: when breakfast was served, how to turn on the heater for the bath, which hours of the day I would have to leave the premises and during which brief periods a bath was permitted (these seemed oddly to coincide), how much notice I should give if I intended to receive a phone call or remain out after 10pm.

There were so many rules that Bryson concluded, 'This was like joining the army.'

And then there was the rationing. I recall between the ages of four and six, taking my ration card to the sweet shop half a mile away down a steep lane at the bottom of the road leading to High Town Road. Scooped from jars, my four ounces of sugar-filled treats were carefully weighed. Food rationing only ended in 1954. The government needed a large standing army because it was trying to cling to its colonies. The tax base was eradicated and we still had commitments on the Continent. All told, it meant that England was poor and the government couldn't expand food production fast enough.

Milk was delivered to the door and so were some groceries. If the grocer's van was seen at the top of the road, it offered no danger because it was slow, as were most cars in the fifties, and we had plenty of time to get onto the pavement. Boys and girls played together tag, hide and seek, French cricket, rounders, sticky toffee, *What's the Time Mr Wolf*, five stones, marbles and hop scotch. Girls alone tended to skip and play two balls up the wall. In the summer holidays we migrated to a grassy slope at the bottom of the road to play cowboys and Indians, soldiers and nurses—all gender stereotyped and unknowingly racist. In August, we picked the blackberries and loganberries growing in the hedges.

My father was one of the first residents in Pomfret Avenue to buy a second-hand car. Unlike today, there were no parked vehicles on the road and we children played together in the street until the sun set, when Mum would call me in, give me hot chocolate and send me to bed. Parenting was a lot easier in those days. The number of minutes parents spend with their children is dramatically higher now than it was in my childhood, rising from 50 minutes in 1965 to 150 minutes in 2016. The world was safe and secure, England was the transcendent nation and my neighbourhood was my universe.

SCONES

½ lb SELF RAISING FLOUR
1 TEASPOON BAKING POWDER
PINCH SALT
1 OUNCE CASTER SUGAR
2 OUNCES BUTTER OR MARG
½ A BEATEN EGG
A LITTLE MILK

RUB BUTTER INTO FLOUR
ADD THE REST OF
INGREDIENTS, THEN EGG
+ MILK.
ROLL OUT & CUT
INTO SCONES. SHOULD BE
9.
BAKE (400)

Mum's well-thumbed scone recipe in her own writing

CHAPTER 2: Cornish Pasties

My parents named their house *Lamorna* after Dad's favourite spot in a three-mile walk from St Buryan, Cornwall. Lamorna Cove was also an inspirational location for Laura Knight, one of the few celebrated female artists of the early twentieth century. My first trip to Cornwall to visit my grandmother was in 1952, aged six and a half. We went from Luton to Paddington Station where we caught the legendary Cornish Riviera to Penzance. I can still feel the shiver of excitement at my first sight of the sea from the carriage window as we sped past Star Cross, Dawlish and Teignmouth, places I later got to know well. I remember clearly that romantic wooded valley leading to the dramatic rocky cove and Lamorna's small sandy beach where I fell in love with Cornwall.

It was intended that my paternal grandmother would greet me when I entered the world. I guess I was difficult even then because I was meant to arrive on 5 December 1945, and yet chose not to. Grannie Elizabeth arrived on the first of the month to help my mother before and after the birth. My brother Ray was fifteen and my brother Michael four and half so there was plenty of work in the home. In working-class homes, there were no machines to help with the washing and cleaning, no easily prepared meals, coal fires had to be cleaned out and lit each day, and a copper boiler to be filled with water by the bucket and heated for the weekly wash.

It's astonishing that in those days there were two postal deliveries and letters almost always arrived the next day. Dad's step-sister Gladys wrote to Grannie every day asking when she was coming home. And so, on 14 December, two days before my birth, she packed her bags and went back to that other country called Kernow, presumably to be welcomed by the waving of the Cornish black and white flag.

Ray and Jean were a handsome bride and groom & I was the little bridesmaid.

Before my first trip to Cornwall to meet this Grannie, my brother Raymond married in Stoke-on-Trent and I was a five-year-old bridesmaid. Ray had spent his National Service stationed near Stafford. Fate determined that at a dance Ray met Jean Turner who, like all Turners, worked in the potteries—she was a painter at Spode. Her glamour captured his heart just as fate had arranged for our father to drive through Stotfold on his black motorbike and, much later in 1963, for my future husband Atam to pull up on an Italian Vespa outside the Gurdwara in Smethwick.

After their wedding Ray and Jean moved in with us while he trained as a policeman. A year later they moved north. My first holiday away from my parents was in 1954 when I stayed with Ray and Jean in Port Vale and as an eight-year-old aunt met their daughter, my niece Lesley. Ray followed in Dad's footsteps in having an allotment but in addition he had a shed where he grew the most delicious mushrooms—a rare treat in the fifties. On that trip Ray took me to Trentham Gardens and bought me a Mr Whippy ice cream—a new experience. Life was changing. And it was sweet.

It was in between Ray's wedding and my holiday in the potteries that I had that first visit to Cornwall to meet my paternal grandmother. She hadn't come to Ray's wedding. I was slow to understand how deprived of love my father had been. My warm-hearted maternal grandparents in Stotfold died when I was six and seven years old so, when I never received a single birthday card, letter or present from my Cornish family, I didn't know it was strange. I was grateful that, a few weeks before Dad died, I could tell him that I loved him.

I have no recollection of my dad's mother ever hugging me or playing with me, but I do recall my first taste of Cornish pasties which she made to a traditional Cornish miner's recipe. Clotted cream from Jersey cows was a delicious surprise, surpassed only by clotted cream ice cream. I drank warm milk straight from the cow. My mother learned Grandma Elizabeth's recipe and growing up, Cornish pasties were one my favourite dishes. Occasionally Mum made a Cornish Clanger to take as a picnic. The savoury filling was at one end and the other end was filled with strawberry jam.

My grandmother's recipe for Cornish Pasties

The rough shortcrust pastry was made using lard. The pastry was rolled out in large 10inch plate size circles and filled and then carefully folded over and the edges twisted so that there were no gaps and brushed with milk or beaten eggs.

The contents

It had to be beef skirt with cubed onions, cubed potatoes and cubed swede with lots of salt and pepper and a couple of tablespoons of water.

The pasties were baked for 10 mins at 200 C.

Then the temperature was lowered to 160 C/gas 4 and cooked for 50 mins.

CHAPTER 3: Corsets, Rulers and Frozen Peas

Some of the best changes I've witnessed in my lifetime were the abolition of the death penalty, the legalisation of homosexuality, the legislation that gave women rights over our bodies and the abolition of physical punishments for children. There were other things as well that were illegal then that just seem punitive now. Like gambling. That was to have consequences for my eldest brother, Ray.

As a police constable he was ordered to go in civilian clothes to a local pub and befriend the landlord in the hope of being invited to a secret poker game. Pubs in those days rarely served food apart from pork pies or packets of pork scratchings; they were mostly drinking places where working men escaped the home. Ray fulfilled the brief and was told to return in his policeman's uniform to arrest the landlord. The problem for Ray was that he liked the guy and didn't see anything wrong in playing cards for money stakes. He gave in his notice. But his police training proved useful when Jean gave birth to their third child. Steven was in a hurry to arrive and Ray ended up delivering his son—at least he'd learned how!

In June 1961, my other brother, Mike, Dad and I made a trip to Southampton. Ray joined us on his motorbike so that he could stay overnight with Uncle Charlie (the Burma veteran) in Petersfield. The following morning he scouted the area and saw for sale a Barnum-and-Bailey circus caravan in a beautiful garden in the village of Sarisbury Green in a private road that led to the Hamble. That trip changed his life because he sold his semi and, with Jean and his three children, moved into it. Jean was told that a naval carpenter had it shipped from America and erected the timbered mobile home himself. They survived living in quite tough conditions while Ray built an attractive house on the site. On the back of the sale of their Luton house, Ray started his first one-man business, making wrought-iron gates, fences and staircases, and never looked back. Real GDP doubled between the early 1950s and the early 1970s, which always helps.

Ray's life choices had consequences for me. It was much later that I realised why Miss East, my teacher in the first year of Hart Hill Junior kept hitting me with a ruler. Unbeknown to me, before Ray met Jean, they'd had a couple of dates. My brother had ended the relationship when he was conscripted. Harry is not a common surname so I guess she put two and two together and connected me to him.

Miss Parker was different. It was her final year teaching, one of those so-called 'surplus women,' who remained single because of the carnage of WW1. The 1921 census counted almost two million more women than men, which caused a short-term flap but in the long term helped the transition in the status of women. I visited Miss Parker in her little terraced house after she retired. She was followed by Mr Greenway who encouraged me. In my final year, Mr Watson divided us into four teams and every day lined us up against the walls for quick-fire arithmetic. Every Friday we had English and arithmetic tests to prepare us for the 11+.

Hart Lane Junior School: Mr Watson's class. I'm fourth from the right at the back. Andrew at the front and Ruth diagonally right behind him.

Ray had no chance of a good secondary education which, before the war, was expensive. When it came in 1945, free secondary education for all consisted of three 'courses'. If you passed the 11+ you attended a grammar school, which opened doors to socio-economic mobility. If you were borderline you could go to a technical school and get a solid vocational training. But the majority of children failed the 11+ and so attended a secondary modern school, synonymous with low expectations and low achievements. A post-code lottery resulted in some towns and cities having as much as 25% of students getting grammar school education, although across Britain, only 10% were working class.

In Luton and Dunstable, an area of mixed socio-economics, 20% of boys, including my brother Michael, went to the two grammar schools for boys. But there was only one for girls. When the results came, thirteen boys had places at Luton Grammar School for boys, but only four girls from seventy at my school (less than 6%) were to have a life-changing education at Luton High School for Girls. I put my success down to Luton Central Library where I could consume books with a ravenous appetite, books my parents would not have been able to buy.

Mike and I were examples of the upward mobility that was possible for those of our generation who passed the 11+ exam. The generation of 1945-1975 was one of enormous class mobility due to changes in government policies and the resulting decline of inequality. In 1945 the richest 0.01% of people in Britain had 123 times the mean national average of income. By 1965 it was halved to 62 times and by 1978 it was at its lowest at 28 times. By 2007, it had once again risen to 144 times and is rising still.

In the fifties and sixties, I watched the purse strings loosen as wallets began to plump out, which meant that tradesmen and women had more work and in turn had more money to spend. Because of the narrowing gap between rich and poor, the mood became one of optimism as people felt they could have a stake in the system.

Vauxhall Motors was doing well and my father had plenty of overtime. It meant we only really saw him on Saturday afternoons and Sundays, and he was tired. If he'd been born fifty years later, his life would have been so different. He was an inventor. When he first trained as a toolmaker it was to make the tools to make the parts to make the cars. General Motors took over Vauxhall and in the fifties they set up a suggestion scheme. There was a £60 prize for any worker whose idea was adopted. £60 was a lot of money in the fifties. Dad won it three times and they suggested he stop being a rectification fitter and join the Research and Development Department. He declined the white-collar job. Even aged ten I had the wisdom to consider it a bad choice. His reasoning was that, because of the overtime, we were enjoying increasing prosperity. To put it another way, my parents thought that being middle class didn't pay.

For the Coronation in 1953, my parents bought a seven-inch TV. Our front room, reserved for special occasions, was packed with neighbours on that day. The rain cleared in time for the street party. Just as well as I was wearing a red, white and blue layered dress made out of PAPER! Street party food was mostly sandwiches, sausage rolls, jammy dodgers and fairy cakes served with orange squash.

The overtime paid for our first fridge. It had a tiny freezer compartment which meant not only ice cream but also a new addition to our diet was possible: frozen peas! Dad was able to buy a second hand car, not a Vauxhall but a little square black Morris 10.

Overtime also meant they could afford to buy my new school uniform, which was not inexpensive. Pomfret Avenue was two-and-a-half miles from my high school. If we had lived three miles away, I'd have qualified for free transport. Paying for the bus was a problem. In wet weather I took it but the rest of the time, I walked or cycled to school. Mostly I walked because, at the junction of Hart Lane and Round Green, I met up with Ruth and later on with an older pupil Effie, and we chatted away as we crossed Popes Meadow, which we called High Town Park, and ambled through Wardown Park—the shortest distance as the crow flew.

I became aware that my parents were more prosperous than Mum's sisters' families. Aunties Freda, Bertha and Phyllis all lived in Letchworth Garden City. Their maiden name was Howard and that was apt because the visionary behind the garden cities movement was the fabulously named Ebenezer Howard. Homes heated by coal fires led to life-threatening winter smog when you could hardly see a hand in front of your face. Ebenezer Howard wanted to build smokeless, slum-less cities in which factories, green spaces, workers' housing and shops were in their own distinct areas. Letchworth was the first garden city created from land acquired in 1903.

My mum and her sisters were beneficiaries of Ebenezer's vision. Instead of becoming servants they went to work in a spotless, light-filled and friendly factory in Letchworth. The building that once housed the Spirella corset factory still stands. The arts and crafts style factory included baths, showers, a gym, a library and a room for bicycle repairs.

Years ahead of its time, Spirella revolutionised the relationship between the workforce and the company. There was a ban on alcohol but that wouldn't have mattered to the Howards who were Methodists or Salvationists and, for most of the time, were tee-totallers. After work the girls were able to shower before cycling the two miles back to Stotfold and their home without a bathroom. Bath there was a tin one in front of the range on which they heated water in large pans.

That British desire to have your own castle was to transform the country I'd grown up in from socialist values to Margaret Thatcher's vision of a property-owning democracy. Although I mourned the loss of community spirit that went with it, I understood why it was attractive to working class people like my aunts and uncles who, unlike me, voted for her.

Battered fish (cod or haddock), mashed potatoes and frozen peas with parsley sauce.

For my mother the secret of good fish was simple: it had to be FRESH. She bought it and cooked it on the same day. When they retired to Cornwall, it was even better because she shopped from the fishermen. She didn't have black pepper in the fifties - only white.

Season the fish and dust lightly with flour; this enables the batter to stick to the fish.

To make the batter, sift the flour and a pinch of salt into a large bowl and beat in the water. The batter must be thick enough to coat the back of a wooden spoon. (You can use beer instead of water.)

Coat the fillets with the batter. Carefully place in the hot fat and cook for 8-10 minutes until golden and crispy. To me it would be anathema but Mum often fried in lard or beef dripping.

Remove from the pan, drain and sit on a baking sheet lined with greaseproof paper.

Frozen peas: no microwaves in the late fifties so she boiled them with salt and sprigs of mint.

Parsley Sauce

Make a simple white sauce and add heaps of finely chopped parsley and season with salt and pepper. Mum used only part milk for her white sauce; she added a little stock from the boiled potatoes. Fat again: no olive oil or rapeseed oil in those days. She used lots of butter in the mash and to make the white sauce.

CHAPTER 4: School Dinners, Youth Hostelling and Foreign Parts

My first Luton High School photo aged 12

Luton High School for girls was unusually large with over 1,000 pupils and, Hogwarts-style, divided into houses. Darling House into which the sorting hat placed me was named after Grace Darling who was once a celebrated heroine. On 7 September 1838, she risked her life to rescue the stranded survivors of the wrecked steamship *Forfarshire*. So the sorting hat did its job well.

I had my first experience of the school dinners that would be the main meal of my day for the next seven years. The menu was not so different from my mother's. You didn't have the choices children get today but the fresh ingredients were possibly better? Shepherd's pie and cabbage, chops served with mashed potatoes and carrots and a ploughman's salad on Thursdays, and fish and chips and peas on Fridays. Rissoles, spam fritters and ham and pineapple made appearances. Desserts included stewed fruit, Eve's pudding, rice puddings, fruit pies, and custard and ice cream with tinned fruit or jelly.

I tell young people that chance plays an underappreciated role in life. The headmistress made a decision without which I would not be writing this book. I did well in the end-of-year exams and was put in her new creation, a class called Transitus. Students who wished to apply for Oxford and Cambridge had to stay on an extra year after A Levels to take their entrance exams. In an industrial town like Luton, few girls were in a position to do that. Eileen Evans, the headmistress, believed that if the brighter girls could sit O Levels after 4 years aged fifteen and A levels aged seventeen, they'd be more likely to stay on to take Oxbridge entrance. That was how I came to take my O Levels at fifteen. I have no doubt that if I had taken them at sixteen, like most girls of my background, I'd have left school and started work. Because of Eileen Evans, I studied for A levels and became the first in my family to enter higher education.

Mrs Evans was forward thinking in other ways. As I became a stroppy teen, I was not keen on the uniform, especially that hat. Walking home up Popes Meadow, I enjoyed tossing it in the air and jumping on it. Maybe Mrs Evans was watching because ours was the first grammar school to allow sixth formers to wear clothes of their choice. And her decision even made it into Vogue. Editor Audrey Withers complained that the uniforms give British girls scant chance to:

> blossom into pretty, well-dressed young. Recently one girls' school
> decided that a modest blossoming might not bring on moral blight:
> Headmistress Eileen Evans of Bedfordshire's Luton High School
> announced that her sixth-formers (mostly 17-year-olds) could chuck
> their uniforms, put on regular dresses, nylons and makeup-but no

jewellery. Encouraged by this move, one clothier last week invited headmistresses to a showing of remodelled uniforms, including gym slips with 'a hint of fashion line...'

I was usually attentive and well behaved and most years was given an award. There was one year I missed out—the year I wrote on the Latin mistress's white boots in black ink. My school leaving report shows that it wasn't that I disliked languages-only Latin. I didn't understand why we had to learn a dead language; it seemed an utter waste of time. I was given a detention, unusual in the Transitus form, but managed to persuade the headmistress to let me drop Latin. Some subjects are wasted on the young. Thirty years later, I'd have appreciated Latin for its own sake. When teaching children whose parents haven't academic experience, my advice is to explain clearly the reasons why the subject is important and relate it to the individual. Working-class children like me were and, I think, remain pragmatic.

Unlike my brother Michael, I was not talented at sport. But I had passions beyond reading. As president of the debating society in 1962-3, we began the year debating with boys from the grammar school: '*Sex Equality is Impossible.*' It certainly felt like that at that time. In 1960, Penguin Books was prosecuted under the Obscene Publications Act for distributing *Lady Chatterley's Lover* by DH Lawrence. And won! We were heading in the direction of the sixties but for most people the sixties happened in the seventies.

Pragmatism meant that I worked every Saturday and most holidays from the age of fourteen at Freeman Hardy and Willis shoe shop. I was paid 2% commission on sales as well as £1 in wages. I enjoyed the independence that came with having my own money. It meant that I could indulge my new interest. In 1957, I watched Elvis Presley on our seven-inch TV singing *Loving You* and fell for him. I bought the 78rpm record. When I left home Mum, who was a good parent but a fanatical housewife, cleared out my record collection. If I'd still had it – I'm not a great thrower out of things—it would be worth a lot today.

My Saturday job gave me the freedom to enjoy what was on offer. A coffee bar with a coin-operated Wurlitzer juke box opened on the high street. Not far away was Farmers, a record shop with sound booths where you could listen to the disc before you decided to buy. Opposite was a Sainsbury's where you queued at each counter waiting to be served. Despite glimmers of glamour, we were still a long way from today's world. Coffee was not rationed during and after the war, but the only coffee I'd seen in my house was Camp Coffee, a bottled chicory-flavoured liquid substitute, which I quite rightly loathed. Tea was the drink of choice in most homes. The Harlequin coffee bar, where some of us headed after school, was serving the latest must-have: frothy coffee. This cool place where rockers gathered still served traditional items like toasted tea cakes, but not spam or canned corned beef. It wasn't until I met Simonetta Agnello Hornby in 1971, that I tasted espresso.

Young people today will find it hard to imagine the freedom we enjoyed. From the age of ten, every holiday I headed off with friends on our bikes. Mum provided a packed lunch, usually egg or fish paste sandwiches and an apple or banana and a flask of tea or squash and enough cash to buy an ice cream. My parents didn't have a landline until 1970 and mobile phones were only in the fantasies of Isaac Asimov. They'd have no idea where I was and only an approximate idea of when I'd return. I remember when my brother Mike was bought home in an ambulance. He'd cycled to Windsor with friends and gone for a swim in the Thames where he'd cut an artery on a broken bottle.

Aged thirteen, with my friend Ruth Ennis, I went youth hostelling. I was the only girl in at least a square mile of our house to go to Luton High School. That was why Ruth, who lived about a mile away, was the only pupil I met outside of school or school activities. Her parents had a phone. They helped her with the planning. We cycled first to Jordan's youth hostel in Buckinghamshire, not far from Beaconsfield. When Justin and Amita (they're still a long time in my future) moved to nearby Chalfont St Peter, I took a nostalgic diversion to see it and was surprised that it was as I remembered.

The second day was a seventy-mile ride to Charlbury. From High Wycombe heading north on the A40 we enjoyed an exhilarating ride down Telegraph Hill except you didn't need to cycle because it was steep and long and we were approaching Tetsworth before we needed to pedal hard. Today you would put your life at risk cycling on the A40 among the fast cars and heavy lorries. At three in the afternoon we reached the edge of Oxford and turned right onto the ring road so didn't get a view of the dreaming spires. Twenty miles later we finally arrived at the Cotswold town of Charlbury. I was more tired and hungry that I'd ever been in my life. I can't remember what we ate, only dropping off the second I put my head on the pillow.

The next day, we enjoyed a doddle of only thirty-three miles to Badby in Northamptonshire. Pushing our bikes up the hill we passed a little cottage. A smiling lady, her grey hair tied back in a bun, sat outside and we said 'Hello'. She called us over and the aroma of freshly baked bread wafted out of her kitchen. She invited us in and served us slices still warm and with lashings of butter. Behind her was a glossy black range like my maternal grandmother's. The perfume was familiar; it was how I remembered Grannie Eliza, for she too had baked delicious bread. Later I tasted fragrant loaves in France and my first encounter with stone-baked Sicilian pizza in Mose in 1976 was memorable. This was special because the best food memories are bound up with people and places. There's an emotional power connected to food that involves all the senses and none is more intense than the smell and the steam, the texture and the taste of freshly baked bread. Added to that is the human warmth and connection that comes with sharing.

Mike had left school after A levels to work in a bank. His ambition had been to study at Loughborough and become a PE teacher, but he was persuaded that higher earnings was a better idea. Mike, like Ray, had an adventurous spirit and in 1960, it was the Rome Olympics so he and two friends went and had a great time. Unknown to us, Mike had been in touch with the Australian Embassy. In the New Year, he told the family he'd been accepted as a new Australian.

Like the UK after the war, Australia needed immigrants. Australia only wanted white immigrants and was prepared to pay for them. Mike's six-week fully catered journey by sea would cost him the princely sum of £10; the rest was paid by the Australian government.

At that point, I hadn't come face to face with a single Black or Brown person, but I was aware of the Windrush generation and had seen on TV how Mosley's Black Shirts stirred up hatred in Notting Hill. I'd watched a Panorama programme on Peter Rackman, the slum landlord, who exploited the industrious new arrivals. Enoch Powell had been to the West Indies to recruit nurses, and British Rail and the post office had done the same thing. When immigrants arrived in greater numbers than expected, the government turned off the warm welcome and even tried to profile them as criminals in an effort to encourage them to go 'home'.

This was the start of a distressing time for Black Britons. Even when they were victims of crimes and tried to report it to police, they were often treated as criminals. In 1981, they marched to Fleet Street angered by the horrific death of thirteen teenagers in a fire in New Cross which was half-heartedly investigated—no one was ever charged for arson and the media mostly ignored it. Arriving outside The Daily Mail and the Sun, the marchers were greeted with chants and banners saying, 'Blacks Go Home'.

The problem was that these new arrivals had been taught that they were indeed coming home to the Mother Country. Steve McQueen's 2021 BBC TV series, Small Axe, is a brilliant portrayal of that time. The realisation that Black lives didn't matter was obvious in the late fifties, early sixties.

Mum wouldn't go to Southampton to see Mike off. If he wanted to return, it would cost £450. My first teaching salary was £660 per annum. In the sixties it would take a long time to save that kind of money. Entirely reasonably, our mother didn't believe that she would ever see him again.

Can there be a day that determines the rest of your life? June 8,

1961 was a turning point in both my brothers' lives because on that spring day, Ray put an offer on the Sarisbury Green mobile home and that would lead to him becoming an independent business man. Michael was nineteen years old, travelling alone, knowing no one in Australia and without a job but with a big grin on his face believing in a future of discovery. After we had said our goodbyes, I waved energetically as he climbed the gangplank onto the *FairSky*. The next time I would hear his voice was on my wedding day.

Later that year I enjoyed my first journey outside England. The Religious Education teacher, Miss Dorling, organised for a group of us to go on a cruise to Spain and Portugal. MS Devonia was a troopship in WW2 and it hadn't changed much. I guess they assumed transporting children was not so different to soldiers. Cruising 2019 style is a couple of centuries ahead of MS Devonia 1961. Crossing the Bay of Biscay I thought I'd made a mistake—it was no fun being seasick.

Spain and Portugal, at the time under the dictatorships of Franco and Salazar, were a world away from the countries they are today. Tourists in Vigo, Corunna and Lisbon were not in abundance: in fact, we were the only ones. Female unchaperoned tourists were fair game. Everywhere we went we were followed by groups of men wolf whistling, although they felt more a nuisance than a threat. Almost all meals were on board and we were given packed lunches for the days on land so I didn't get to sample Spanish or Portuguese food.

I was learning German badly and had a penfriend called Brigitte who lived in Aalen near Stuttgart. In 1963, my school friend Angela and I headed for Baden Württemberg to spend two weeks with our pen pals. This was a real eye opener. Brigitte's family lived in a flat but compared to my home it was modern, light and airy with central heating, constant hot water, a washing machine and a SHOWER!

Brigitte had visited us the previous year. She enjoyed Luton and London but was not taken with my beloved Cornwall. We stayed at Dad's cousins' delightful B&B in a farm house overlooking Sennen Cove. Cousins Hilda and Herbert were lovely people who generously accommodated us for free but needed our room for a booking on the final night of our visit. So they sent us to stay with an old lady who lived a few fields away. The cottage had no electricity, only gas light, and Calor gas for cooking, which was common in farms and hamlets in Cornwall at that time. The cottage had no flushing toilet only an Elsan chemical one at the bottom of the garden. When I saw the Zieman's apartment, I understood why Brigitte had not been impressed.

Me, Brigitte and Angela in Stuttgart

I was struck by how prosperous Germany felt compared to England—the Germans after all had lost the war. The reason was easy to see. Their old industries had been destroyed to be replaced by cutting-edge, new factories. After the war, the British controlled the Ruhr and put into practice a fine industrial-relations policy with unions represented on boards. The result was that, unlike in England, there wasn't a class divide between management and workers. Tragically we couldn't create the same systems here. If we had, the de-industrialisation of the Thatcher era wouldn't have been so severe. German vocational training was and remains world beating. Unlike in the UK, where a knowledge of Latin and Greek was valued over all other, Germans respected skilled manual labour. No wonder they were (and are still) doing well!

Many Brits were anti-German but I felt no such animosity. Germans were facing up to their past and creating a democracy. Aged eleven, I watched the World at War, which included scenes from the liberation of Belsen. I understood the horrors but most of my generation wanted to create a better world, one of peace and prosperity for all. We turned our face to the future.

Receiving a prize for achievements in RE. The headmistress Eileen Evans is farthest away. The deputy head, my Maths teacher, Miss Ling (looking bored), was talked about as being in a lesbian relationship with the music teacher with whom she lived. No one seemed to mind.

1961 Southampton Docks saying farewell to Mike before he boarded the FairSky.
Mum wouldn't come with us—she couldn't bring herself to say 'Goodbye.' From
left: Raymond, Uncle Charlie, me, my cousin Pat, Dad, Mike
and cousin David

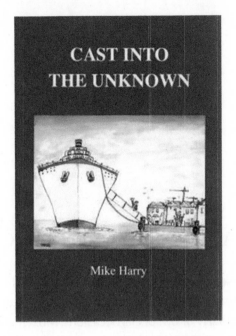

Book Cover of Cast Into the Unknown: My brother Mike's memoir about being a £10 pom

Recipes

Spam fritters: Why waste your time?
Wurst: My first introduction to charcuterie. Best just bought from a deli!
Homemade bread: Now that is worthwhile for the aroma alone.

CHAPTER 5: Faith Served Up Cold

My lifetime has seen a decline in religious affiliation. In the fifties over 80% of the British population was Christian, and attended church or chapel either regularly or on special occasions. Most married in a church and had a Christian burial. In the last census barely 50% of population identified as Christian. In a school book, *Land of the Temples* published in 1882, cremation was cited as an abominable heathen practice. By 2020, the Hindu practice of cremation is the choice of 77% of the population.

My grandchildren find it hard to understand how large religion loomed in my childhood. The biggest impact was on Sundays when no shops could open and entertainment was taboo. On Sundays, we were not allowed out to play; for children not to observe the Sabbath brought shame on a respectable working-class family. On Sunday mornings after a traditional English fry up, I was sent to Sunday school. The church was a mile's walk away and I'd return with a large appetite for Mum's perfect roast dinner, my favourite of the week. It was hard work for her because cleaning the oven and the pans afterwards was not as easy as it is today. Dad sometimes helped but Sunday was a time he could do gardening and minor repairs about the house.

In the afternoon I read, occupied myself with *Things to Make and Do* from the Children's Encyclopaedias or played cards and board games with Michael. From eleven years of age onwards, there was homework to do. Once we owned a car, every six weeks we'd head off for tea with family in Stotfold or Letchworth—or as a special treat go to Petersfield for the weekend and stay over with Uncle Charles, Auntie Eva and their children.

Tragedy hit when our favourite cousin, Basil, died aged fifteen from a strangulated hernia, which is unthinkable today. I was nine. For both my grandmother's and Basil's funerals I was not allowed in the church. I vividly remember both occasions; the motive was to protect me but the reality was that I felt excluded.

Although my parents rarely went to church themselves, they sent me to Sunday School because, I suspect, they wanted a bit of peace. But Dad was influenced by the Wesleyan culture that was strong in West Cornwall. He rarely drank alcohol and my only memento of him, apart from photographs, are his Left Book Club books, not surprising because the Labour Party grew out of Methodism. He may have left school aged fourteen but his reading was not dumbed down.

Faith, Reason and Civilisation by Harold Laski
The Unity of Europe by Hilda Monte
Battle Hymn of China by Agnes Smedley
The Black Man's Burden by John Burger
Mission to Moscow by Joseph E Davies

Myself, I've never shaken off Methodist pragmatism. My favourite aunt, Aunt Alice, had a profound influence on me. Like my mother she left school aged fourteen to work at the Spirella corset factory but she went with my grandfather to the Salvation Army meetings and not with Grandma Eliza to the Methodist Church.

The Salvation Army was an early example of gender equality in action. Alice set off to Camberwell Green in London to train as an officer and by the age of twenty she was running a hostel in the Gorbals, in Glasgow. If Salvation Army officers want to marry, it has to be to a fellow officer because they are usually moved on every five years. She met Scottish-born Lesley Drummon in Glasgow. He was better educated and when I knew them, he worked at the SA headquarters as its treasurer. I stayed with them in Woodford Green and used their home as a base to explore London for the first time. Alice encouraged me when I became sincerely Christian around the age of fourteen, and she provided me with an example of a woman who could speak and be listened to.

I have been asked, and even wondered myself, from where I got my commitment to social justice. Was it a family thing? To a degree, yes. I'd like to give credit to Aunt Alice, but it was also the spirit of the times: we believed that we could change the world for the better. I regret that that attitude now seems foolishly optimistic but modern negativity also creates its own self-fulfilling prophecy.

When I was fifteen, an evangelist came from the USA to teach us how to reach out. A group of us of all ages from Round Green Methodist Church attended his courses at a larger middle-class establishment in Montrose Avenue near Wardown Park. He showed films of a prosperous South Carolina church and how they organised their outreach. I noticed there was not a single black face in the film, although there were black people in the street shots. Afterwards I asked him why. He replied, 'They have their own churches.'

'But you do get together?' I asked.

He didn't answer. I realised that this seemingly open and warmhearted man would turn away a dark-skinned Jesus if he turned up at his church.

When I went to work in Smethwick for a year before college, I started going to the homes of some Sikh girls and had my first exposure to Indian food. They suggested I go to the Sikh temple on Sunday mornings. I loved it because they fed you Punjabi vegetarian food for free! This was my first encounter with the revolutionary idea that a main meal didn't have to include meat. A horrendous aspect of the caste system was not sharing a meal or wanting to be touched by lower or non-caste people. Eating together, Sikhs tasted equality.

Food and fasting plays a significant role in many religions. In Christianity, I knew the sharing of bread (or food) as 'communion' and in Sikhism sharing a meal felt empathetic with extended families taking turns to cook for the community in memory of a loved one. I have invented a word for it *communessence*. If Shakespeare can add hundreds of words and phrases to the language, can't I contribute one?

Wouldn't it be great if the idea of *communessence*, of people of all backgrounds sharing a meal as equals, was possible? There would be rows as well as laughter, but it would be harder to label people as 'other' and not part of our particular herd. Bertrand Russell said, 'Collective fear stimulates herd instinct, and tends to produce ferocity towards those who are not regarded as members of the herd.'

How better to dissolve fear than through sharing the food of love?

After paying for my bedsit in Handsworth and bus fares to Smethwick, I didn't have much money for food. In the dining hall, I asked the two turbaned young men sitting opposite us to tell me about Sikhism and they did. I felt welcomed at the Gurdwara so, that evening, I asked the deaconess of the church I'd joined if I could invite some Sikhs the following week. She agreed. We sat together through the service and afterwards I introduced them to the deaconess and she chatted to them for a while. We helped ourselves to coffee and biscuits but **NO ONE** came and spoke to them. The following week I asked some members of the congregation why. The answer was, '*Indians coming to live in Smethwick are devaluing our property.*'

I didn't go back.

A couple of weeks later, I met up with a guy from my church in Luton. Derek was in Handsworth training to become a Methodist minister. I got to know him as a fellow student; we were both training to be lay preachers. That's how serious I was. The West Indians in Handsworth were mostly enthusiastic Christians—a bit too enthusiastic for my temperament but I liked them. I wanted to find an integrated church. I asked Derek what they were doing to connect with the West Indians and which church was mixed. It was the same one-world-white one-world-black scenario as in South Carolina.

The publication in 1963 of the controversial *Honest to God* by John Robinson, Bishop of Woolwich, was headline news and prompted heated debate. He challenged traditional theology, reinterpreting some aspects of Christianity like the idea of resurrection in a Buddhist manner. I wasn't the only one rethinking my faith. I questioned whether Jesus was God but I never doubted the wisdom and goodness of what he taught. It wasn't the doubt which drove me away but the hypocrisy. Some of the great souls of my lifetime were and are religious people, and they inspire me to savour spirituality. Just after I finished this memoir, Desmond Tutu died and he is someone I hope the world will never forget. Here is a poem I wrote that celebrates the joyfulness and mischief of his spirituality.

Great Souls

They named Gandhi, the Mahatma:
the first of the great souls in my lifetime.
Martin Luther King and Gandhi taken by bullets fired with hate.
Mandela and Tutu mercifully died in their beds.
All deserve the title.

One remains with us: the Dalai Lama
No surprise that he and Desmond liked each other
Their warm and infectious personalities exuded humour
Impish together as well as exemplars of love.
The depth of ages disguised by childlike delight.

Keep alive the memory of that irreverent Reverend
Dancing and joking down the aisle
In response to persecution.
Humanity needs his spirit

The courage, the laughter and the tears
Of Desmond Tutu.

My faith may have been served up cold but at the same time, in November 1963, I had my first taste of heat at the Gurdwara. A daal was always on the menu. Here is my daughter-in-law Amita's recipe, a favourite with our family.

Amita Vetta's recipe for Daal

(It feeds a lot of people so popular at Gurdwaras)

Ingredients:

Black daal, kidney beans canned tomatoes (or passata) butter
Onions, ginger, garlic, salt and spices as indicated.

Boil a pack of black daal, cover and simmer.
Add two teaspoons garam masala and lots of salt and whole green chillies.
In a separate saucepan fry whole cumin seeds in oil. Once they pop add 2 chopped onions 3 cloves of crushed garlic and 4 inches of chopped ginger. Fry until soft and golden brown. Add the above mixture to the daal.
Add two tins of chopped tomatoes and three tins of kidney beans.
Add one pack of butter.
Simmer on a very low heat for 5 hours stirring and adding water from time to time. Don't let the daal stick to the bottom.
Before serving check for taste and add salt, masala and chilli powder if required. This will serve a lot of people but leftovers freeze well.

CHAPTER 6: Smethwick 1963/4

I'd never seen a university and knew no one who had a degree. That was not surprising because, in the early sixties, only seven percent of the population enjoyed higher education and a large majority of students were male. In 1963, the Robbins Report laid out the bare facts about the lack of access. It recommended the establishment of more universities and polytechnics, and the Wilson Government, elected in 1964, would implement Robbins' recommendations. This was part of a larger economic push to modernise the workforce for a higher order of industrial development. Polytechnics would have an impact on my future.

While I had no concept of 'university', I understood a teacher's role. I wasn't sure if it was the career that I wanted but my parents thought it a good idea and supported my choice. There was a problem: I was too young. I was only seventeen when I left school with A levels so what to do for a year? I had heard of a newish organisation called Voluntary Service Overseas (VSO). The influence of my brothers, who had powerful appetites to travel, plus my reading, had given me itchy feet. I applied to join VSO and was called for an interview with Alec and Mora Dickson in their apartment (also VSO headquarters) in Mortlake, London.

It was only when I was there that it dawned on Alex that I wasn't yet eighteen and again my age disqualified me. He came up with an alternate suggestion. He had just founded Community Service Volunteers (CSV), that worked in the UK. Teachers, even unqualified ones, were needed for a sudden influx of the children of immigrants in Smethwick in the West Midlands. The steel factories in the West Midlands were keen to recruit immigrants and Punjabis had responded to their advertisements. They had a particular motivation.

When it was inevitable that Britain had to leave India in 1947, a new party to rival Gandhi's Congress was founded: the Muslim League led by Jinnah. This suave, unreligious man believed Muslims should not be dominated by a Hindu majority. The British responded by partitioning India between the predominately Muslim areas in the North, which became Pakistan, and the rest. The flash point where the line was drawn was in the Punjab. It's estimated that a million people were killed in the partitioning of the country. It was ethnic cleansing on a vast scale. That's why the immigrants who responded to the offer of jobs in heavy industry in the Midlands were mostly from the divided Punjab.

Strict new immigration rules were being talked about, and the men who had come to work in the iron works thought this could be their last chance to bring their families to the UK. The immigrants were not from the well-educated, English-speaking elite castes; they mostly spoke only Punjabi. The schools, confronted with pupils who could not speak English, had no experience of dealing with the situation. Alex explained that I would be given some training in the techniques of teaching English as a second language.

Going to Smethwick was to be another one of those chance events that shaped my life. If Eileen Evans hadn't created a Transitus class I wouldn't have taken my A levels. If I'd been eighteen when I applied to VSO, I'd have been sent to Zambia. Either way I wouldn't have met Atam and my family would not be here. How contingent are all our lives!

I packed my one and only suitcase and Dad drove me to Birmingham. CSV had booked me a room at a hostel called the Girls Friendly Society.

When I saw the small cell-like curtain-less and wardrobe-less room for two, I knew I wouldn't stop for long.

Jane was a fellow CSV volunteer. She was the daughter of a wealthy businessman in Grimsby and not only could she drive, but she owned a car. In those days, there were only approximately five million vehicles on the road and that included commercial vehicles. They were expensive to buy and expensive to run. When Jane and I met on the first day of the course, she suggested we find somewhere to share accommodation.

A lady had advertised in the Smethwick Telephone: a double room with full board at a price I could just afford to share at £7 6s a week. The landlady was young, not an old fusspot worrying that we might spill tea on her carpet. We congratulated ourselves on the lucky find. But by the fourth week, we'd handed in our notice and found self-catering accommodation in nearby Handsworth. Our darling landlady had started telling us stories when she served our evening meal: disturbing stories. Dinnertime conversation became increasingly peculiar as she regaled us with her escapades. We made alternate arrangements after a meal when she gleefully told us about how she been expelled from school when she stabbed a girl in the eye with a pair of scissors.

Ten of us were being prepared to work in different secondary schools in the borough. Graham Newis was a graduate teacher who had just left university with a degree in French. There were two other qualified teachers. The rest of us were unqualified, but Jane and I were the only trainees who were legally 'children'. In those days twenty-one was the age of adulthood, when you could vote and marry without your parent's consent.

Teaching English as a foreign language (TEFL) has become a big business, so today's TEFL graduates would be amazed by what faced us in 1963 in Smethwick. There were NO textbooks designed for use in the UK. Our instructor learned the techniques of teaching English as a second language to a mixed language class at the University of Michigan. He provided us with copies of *English for New Australians*.

It was bizarre: the books contained maps of Australia and pictures of jumping kangaroos. (A few years later Longman's published a British version of it.)

After four weeks of training, I was assigned to Smethwick Hall Secondary Modern School for Boys each morning and Smethwick Hall Secondary Modern School for Girls in the afternoon. The heads of each school took different approaches.

At the boys' school, I had twenty-two pupils from Pakistan, India, Cyprus and Poland to teach all morning. In the afternoon they joined ordinary classes for science, sport and art. The girls' school handled it better. I was sent groups of seven or eight girls for an hour each day and then they returned to the English-speaking environment of a normal classroom.

I was also witnessing the growing poison in Smethwick. I'd become an avid newspaper reader early in life so I bought the *Smethwick Telephone*. It was unlike any other local newspaper. Every week its front page promoted fear of immigrants. The paper alleged criminality by immigrants and claimed that minorities had huge rates of VD, TB and leprosy, and lived in unsanitary conditions. A typical example of a front-page headline was *Eighteen Beds come out of a House in Vicarage Road*. Finding accommodation was tough at a time when notices saying *No Blacks No Irish No Dogs* were not uncommon. Squeezing in with men from your village had often been the only option. This story interpreted multi-occupation as the way immigrants lived as if they had a choice.

You couldn't live or work in the borough without hearing the slogan, *If you want a nigger for a neighbour vote Labour.* It was encouraged by Don Finney, a supporter of Peter Griffiths, the Conservative candidate for the 1964 general election. Mr Finney soon became a Conservative councillor. He was reported saying, 'I had a wonderful fortnight's holiday. Did not see a single nigger!' *and* 'There is a black invasion swamping this country and in Marshall Street, we are trying to control it by preserving the balance of coloured and whites. It is a brave effort by local residents.'

He was referring to a plan to set up an 'All White Association', starting in Marshall Street, where only nine households were of Indian ancestry. Finney and Griffiths launched a campaign to purchase houses on the street to prevent immigrants from buying them. He had been saying and writing similar inflammatory comments since 1961, and the Smethwick Telephone's editorials tended to agree with him. Questioned on the proposal Finney said, 'The truth behind the Marshall Street story is that an 84-year-old widow, living alone in a house was literally worried to death by Indians. After that the people in Marshall Street came to the council for protection.'

A retired GP, Dr Dhani Prem, asked for evidence and of course Councillor Finney didn't reply. So the doctor visited Marshall Street to talk to residents. The people he met were distressed that Finney had used this woman's natural death to promote his views. Her relations were embarrassed. Dr Prem then went to the police to see if there had been any reported incidents. The reply was, 'We have no record on our files of any complaint by or about this old lady. I am rather surprised, in view of what is alleged, that no one reported these goings on to us.'

I can quote these dialogues and many more like them thanks to Dr Prem keeping a meticulous record of the events leading up to Griffith's victory in the 1964 election. He privately published *The Parliamentary Leper (Colour and British Politics)* in 1965 and gave Atam and me a signed copy.

I'm sorry to quote those disgusting remarks, including the 'n' word, but without them, it is hard to communicate that vicious atmosphere. Unsurprisingly, the vile propaganda provoked violence. Petrol bombs were thrown into an Indian shop. Houses where Indian immigrants lived had windows smashed. These incidents were not condemned by Peter Griffiths. Being a primary school headmaster in those days he commanded respect. I'd read William Shirer's *Rise and Fall of the Third Reich* and it felt to me that I was witnessing the demonisation of a minority group in the same manner that Hitler had vilified minorities in thirties Germany. What could a soon-to-be eighteen-year-old girl do?

That year in Smethwick squeezed the last drops of innocent joy from my childhood. From then on, I was catapulted into a frightening adult world.

Graham Newis came to me about an Indian maths teacher at Holly Lodge Grammar School for Girls who wanted to start a multi-racial youth club to diffuse tension. 'Would I help?' I sent a message via Graham that I would be at the Gurdwara on Sunday and could meet this teacher at 2pm. So it was that on the last Sunday in October 1963, I was on the steps outside the classical portico of what had once been a Congregationalist church when Atam drove up on an Italian Vespa. Pure sixties cool. As he took off his helmet and looked at me, I couldn't but notice his large, deep-brown eyes. I didn't stand a chance!

I didn't look at him and think: there's a brown-skinned man who is also good-looking. I didn't think: my but that Indian sure looks hot on that Vespa. I didn't think: Atam is more light-skinned than many Indians I've already met.

I didn't think at all. Not of the colour of his skin. Nor of his nationality. Nor of his ethnicity. Any of those things that others may have thought when they met Atam, I didn't. My response was more physical than that.

We rented a gym where it was possible to play basketball and table tennis and music. Gender roles being what they were in those days my assignment was the catering: drinks, biscuits and crisps. No one questioned that, certainly I didn't at the time. Starting the youth club was not simple. Recruiting boys of most skin tones wasn't difficult, and I recruited a few white girls from school, but recruiting Asian girls was a challenge. Atam had the tough task of persuading some parents to let their daughters attend. Because of his academic qualifications and because some Punjabi families knew of his eldest brother, Kundan, who had been imprisoned during the Quit India Movement, they gave him a hearing. They only agreed if we promised that the girls wouldn't talk to the boys. The best we could do was let the girls and boys play table tennis and basketball separately but even then, some of the

Indian girls only wanted to watch. It wasn't the most exciting club and it died a death when we left Smethwick.

The outdoor Saturday morning activities were more successful and *The Birmingham Post* reported on one of them. Unlike *The Smethwick Telephone*, the *Post* was a fair, tolerant and balanced publication, that tried to report facts and not rumours, or what we now know as 'Fake News', like the made-up scare story set in Marshall Street.

THE BIRMINGHAM POST, MONDAY, DECEMBER 9, 1963

Club carries out its first social work

Members of the Smethwick Youth Service Club who cut the front-garden hedges of some of the houses in Vicarage Road, Smethwick, yesterday. This was their first attempt at social work.

White and Indian teenagers helped to trim the hedges under the supervision of Mr. Atam Vetta, a 30-year-old Smethwick schoolmaster, who founded the club. His plan is that it should be multi-racial and not only provide the usual youth facilities but also carry out social service projects. The hedging was in response to requests by some of the Vicarage Road residents.

For some weeks the club had only Indian boys as members. Membership has now reached 45. About 15 of them are white youths.

The secretary is a white youth, and the treasurer an Indian. Mr. Vetta is being helped by two white youth leaders.

The club, which moves on

The Birmingham Post 1963—Graham Newis on left and me second on right.

Atam and I started to meet every Sunday. He was living in a bedsit in Edgbaston opposite Birmingham University. I wanted to know his story. I was still the same curious girl who gobbled up exotic tales. I was like Desdemona about whom Othello said would come 'greedy to hear tales of adventure, sorrow and suffering. *She loved me for the dangers I had passed and I loved her that she did pity them.*'

How could I not feel sorry for Atam? His mother had died when he was only two. His father, Mela Ram, ran a small business buying and selling. By the standards of the village (named Warburton, after a British officer) they were not poor. Atam's oldest brother Kundan was for a long time the only boy from the village to matriculate. He went to Lahore to train to be a doctor in Ayurvedic and western medicine. During his five-year course he joined an anti–British rule protest and was sent to prison for nine months.

Atam's recollection of the marriage of his oldest sister, Sumitra, flags up the heart of the problem for women in India: the cost of weddings!

My father arranged Sumitra's marriage with Anant Ram who lived in a village about 150 miles from Warburton. The wedding party was to stay for two days but on the third day they missed the 8 am train and had to be fed for another day and a half. To pay for it all, my father borrowed money against his house. Regrettably, he couldn't save enough money to pay back the interest and his house had to be sold. He rented two rooms in a bigger house for the family. I know what bankruptcy means.

After their mother died, his brother Roshan was sent to one family and Atam, the youngest, and his sister Krishna who was five years older than Atam, were farmed out together. Krishna was his nearest thing to a mother and he loved her dearly. Atam said, 'None of the families we lived with were unkind but we had to earn our keep. After school, I was used like a house boy. Because I was bright, I earned a British scholarship to secondary school. The system was more like Scotland. I matriculated.'

The confident young teenager started to recruit his own band of revolutionaries with a vision of a bright new caste-free India when two tragedies hit the family: the death of their father and partition. Because they were Hindu, his family had to leave what is now Pakistan. They lost everything but at least they escaped with their lives.

The stories Atam tells of the culture in and around Lahore during his childhood is in sharp contrast to the intolerance and violence that has grown insidiously in Pakistan over the last thirty years. The local imam was impoverished and my husband's Hindu family fed his family while helping him set up a shoe shop. Aged eight, Atam regularly minded the shop during the time for prayer. Sikhs and Hindus worshipped in each other's temples, and Muslims, Hindus and Sikhs revered the shrines of Sufi saints. Partition destroyed that tolerant, music-and-dance-loving Sufi culture. Saudi-funded madrassas became common in Pakistan where they teach Wahhabi Islam. Partition caused one of the greatest migrations in human history, as millions of Muslims headed to West and East Pakistan, and millions of Hindus and Sikhs—my husband's family included—headed in the opposite direction.

To begin with, the family headed for Ludhiana in the Punjab. Once you have been forced to uproot, it's not so hard to move again in search of better opportunities. Some of Atam's family settled in Delhi and others in Mumbai and Ambala. The refugees on both sides of the border didn't have it easy.

Kundan, the eldest brother, became the head of the family but was not able to support everyone, so fifteen-year-old Atam had to look after himself. As he told me his story, I began to fall in love with this man. My brothers had self-belief but the determination to get a degree when you were an orphan and rolled cotton reels and tutored small children—anything to earn a few pennies to eat—it was like something out of Dickens.

Atam worked while he studied as an external student for a BA in

Pure Maths at Punjab University. Unlike most externals he not only passed but was awarded a first-class degree. At eighteen my hormones were swirling. Physical attraction is something that overwhelms most teenagers but I felt there was more to it. Atam's determination was special. After getting an MA in Delhi and a Dip Ed, he became a lecturer at a teacher training college in the Punjab. While there, he saw an advertisement for a post in Ethiopia, which came with an American-funded attractive salary. Atam applied. He said,

> When I arrived for the interview there were fifty other candidates. Maybe I came over as rather arrogant to compensate for believing I was not in with a chance. But I was offered the job and the American attaché led me into a vast room with a high ceiling. At the far end was a throne and on it was the Ethiopian ambassador. I was introduced to him so that he could officially approve my appointment.

He saved money during his time there but needed more if he was to pay the fees to study for a PhD in England. So he took a job in a school in Warwickshire. He was welcomed and has only good memories of his time in Nuneaton. A fellow teacher, Richard Moreton, was Atam's best man at our wedding. He told chess jokes in his speech—Knight to Queen 4: Best Move Yet.

Chance comes into the story again. After studying for one year at Birmingham University, Atam realised that he didn't have enough money to maintain himself for a second year. He left with an MEd to add to his MA in Maths and, in August 1963, looked around for a teaching post. One was advertised in nearby Smethwick. He was overqualified but took it. There, in plain matter-of-fact prose, is a summary of his life until the fateful day we met. As our story unfolds, I'll add the seasoning.

We mostly met in Edgbaston and Birmingham city centre where the atmosphere was congenial. We attended performances at the recently founded Midlands Art Centre and walked in Cannon Hill Park.

I was not impressed by my first taste of Atam's cauliflower curry but to be fair, buying a full range of spices was difficult. Tiny jars of Sharman's spice were available in some New Street shops but they were expensive. In Smethwick kitchens, I'd seen huge jars of spices that families brought with them from India. I'd watched as a pupil's mother named spices such as haldi and dhania. It was all prepared free style— nothing was measured or weighed. I came to think of French cooking as classical music and Indian as jazz. The important skill was to know the notes and improvise. Nowadays, Atam's improved cauliflower curry is one of the family's favourites. Our personal life was spiced up little by little, rather than in a great wave of passion.

One Saturday, after a youth club event, we were walking side-by-side in Smethwick when a man stepped in front of us and spat at me. It was then that I realised how Smethwick residents had been taught to see white women who went with men of colour: we were labelled as loose women or prostitutes. Although the Indian community behaved in a civilised manner, many of them held the same opinion.

Our relationship churned with unwanted dilemmas. On our first visit to India in 1973, it was obvious that Atam had lived away for a long time. He had European habits and his Hindi was dated. In England, he never abandoned those aspects of Indian culture that were important to him. He remained a vegetarian, practiced yoga and listened to Indian music. I first heard Lata Mangeshkar and Mohamed Ravi on 78s in the Edgbaston bedsit. If Atam and I were to continue to see each other, in his view, it needed my parents' approval because family in India is not just about the couple. My parents didn't have a telephone so I wrote every week and as Christmas approached, asked if I could bring Atam home.

My parents welcomed Atam and Christmas dinner wasn't a problem. Mum and Dad rarely went in for turkey preferring a chicken, which wasn't as ubiquitous as now. Atam enjoyed Mum's roast parsnips, crispy roast potatoes and home-made stuffing made with fresh herbs. She left some out of the chicken for Atam. He liked her Yorkshire puddings, fragrant gravy, sprouts mashed with butter and cauliflower

cheese made especially for him. She of course made her own traditional Christmas pudding laced with brandy and with old silver sixpenny
pieces cooked inside. Like most people in those days we settled down
to watch the Queen at 3pm. It was fortuitous that our visit went well.

When I remember that Christmas, my love for my parents is poignant.

Once back in Smethwick for the New Year, we forgot the world
around us and marinated. When writing a memoir, that can be read by
your children and grandchildren, what do you say about sex? The first
time is a landmark in everyone's life and how it happens is integral to
the culture and society you live in so I can't ignore it. We all know that
our parents conceived us but rarely like to think about it. And, in the
fifties, we were taught that good girls never ever did it. Despite that,
I didn't spend a lot of time wrestling with the decision. I suspect that
hormones had something to do with the decision. I may be old now but
I can recall what it felt like to need his touch, to revel in it, to want more
at any cost. I didn't feel cheapened or used or traumatised. Instead I
felt gloriously alive.

Atam had read the Kama Sutra and understood that not only men
had desire, and that giving pleasure to a woman was the secret of a
good relationship. That was not common in the UK at that time. Not
long before my first period, my mother handed me a pamphlet about
the facts of life but was not comfortable talking about it. If Mother
hadn't done that, I wouldn't have known about women's reproductive
cycles; there was no sex education in schools then. The contraceptive
pill became available in the UK in 1961 and was to revolutionise
women's lives, but in 1964 it was reserved for married women. Atam
made sure he was equipped. I don't know how. I never asked. As far as
I was concerned, this just made him more perfect in my eyes. When I
entered the volcano and felt the heat and tremors of desire, I had no
idea that this was how it was meant to be. There were no explicit sex
scenes on film or on TV. Just reading about it in print had only recently
become legal. It was like Eve eating the apple for the first time.

I started to stay over with him on Fridays. Jane had a boyfriend and was more sophisticated than I, but was obviously not impressed. Maybe she worried about the age difference between us, although she never discussed that with me. Because I was under twenty-one years of age, she could and did report me to the chief education officer for having a relationship.

In February, I had a letter from Mum. The chief education officer and his wife had knocked on their door. Their purpose was to let my parents know that I was going out with AN INDIAN!!! My wonderful parents replied, much to his surprise, 'Yes, we know. We met Atam at Christmas and like him.'

They'd never left the UK and not grown up knowing people of many nationalities: their tolerance came from empathy. My father made a joke of it. When my brother Michael turned up with his future wife, who is of Chinese ancestry, he said, 'We'll soon be like the United Nations.'

Atam had taken the post in Smethwick at short notice. He was informed that the contract would not be renewed at the end of the year. We were denied the luxury of letting our relationship develop at a steady pace, enjoying life in the moment. We had to make serious decisions. I wanted a career as a teacher and, after a friendly interview at Westminster College, had been accepted to train there. It was easy to agree that I needed to go but our relationship needed to change. Atam's Indian side came to the fore. It was not a romantic proposal where love conquers all. It was about family. He wanted to marry me but only if my parents agreed!

'Without their support, life will be too tough,' he said.

My response was 'yes' but if he wanted to return to India, it would have to be soon while I was young enough to learn Hindi and to adapt to a new life. At Easter, we went to Luton to talk to Mum and Dad.

They appeared pleased but concerned. Dad took me aside in the evening. He said, 'You know we like Atam. He's a good man and will make you a good husband but are you certain that this is what you want?'

He didn't need to explain because of the racist words and deeds I'd witnessed, and I was aware how many people would regard me as immoral for simply being with a man with a different colour of skin.

Back in Birmingham, Atam took me to a jeweller's to pick the engagement ring. He slipped a sapphire surrounded by diamonds and set in 22-carat gold on my ring finger.

But before that, I headed for Brighton for the Young Socialists Conference. It was a heady year because we all believed the UK was in the mood for change. My favourite TV programme was That Was The Week That Was. Britain was becoming less stuffy and this new style of political satire made us ask questions. Scandals like the Profumo Affair and the strengthening Trade Union Movement were nudging the pendulum towards change. The new leader of the Labour Party, Harold Wilson, talked of cutting-edge technology and cultivated an image of modernity that appealed to people who wanted to accelerate democratic change and not be governed by Eton-educated gentry. Cinema, rock and roll, TV and changing fashion were giving people a vision of a society not dominated by class where you had to 'know your place'.

And not everyone was prejudiced. Atam was appointed to George Dixon Grammar school in Birmingham to begin in September. I moved out of the shared flat into a bedsit. The future was looking pretty rosy, because, as Harold Macmillan said in the 1950s, 'We never had it so good'.

Atam's Cauliflower Curry

Atam makes a paste by grinding in a food processor onion, ginger and garlic enough for several curries and freezes some for future use.

Nowadays he uses a mixture of butter and rapeseed oil.

Heat the fat in a saucepan and add a half teaspoon of whole cumin seeds.

Add two tablespoons of the ginger, onion and garlic paste.

Once it is lightly brown and the fat separates add salt, chilli and turmeric to your own taste.

Atam uses chopped fresh tomatoes but canned or passata is fine too.

Stir in the cauliflower which has been broken into small pieces.

Once it is coated add water and leave it to simmer for 20 minutes.

Stir in ground coriander or garam masala and cook for a few more minutes.

Garnish with fresh coriander.

CHAPTER 7: Seretse Khama
and the Parliamentary Leper

We could not hide from reality. Atam's desire to change things came with the suggestion that we should join the Labour Party and campaign for the sitting Labour MP. Labour had been out of power for thirteen years but all the signs pointed to them winning the 1964 election. In Smethwick, however, the outlook was not good.

Patrick Gordon Walker, the sitting MP, was earmarked to be the next Foreign Secretary because the only Labour MPs with experience in Government were him and Harold Wilson. In the Attlee Government, Gordon Walker had been Commonwealth Secretary. That was to be significant.

The idea that a bus needs two people to operate it is from another age when passengers boarded buses quickly and the 'clippie' went from row to row selling the tickets. In 1955, Mr Patel, a well-educated immigrant, was appointed to work as a bus conductor in West Bromwich, which abuts Smethwick. Immediately the Transport and General Workers Union went on strike saying white women workers would not be safe. The dispute was eventually resolved but this is an example of a Trade Union Movement not being free from prejudice. I became aware of the union's attitude because of the Bristol Bus Boycott in1963. On this occasion bus users were encouraged to boycott the buses until they lifted the colour bar. The boycott lasted four months and drew national attention to racial discrimination in Britain.

In 1964 in Smethwick, the Labour Club had a colour bar. Despite that, the party was keen to register the new arrivals and to get them to vote Labour. Most immigrants were manual workers whose English was not good so Atam was welcomed. He could speak Punjabi, Hindi and Urdu and we accompanied Gordon Walker canvassing.

One Saturday canvassing, we were stopped by a white resident who politely asked what Gordon Walker thought about the Nationality Act. The British Nationality Act of 1948 conferred the status of British citizen on all Commonwealth subjects and recognised their right to work and settle in the UK, and to bring their families with them. It was the reason that the Indian immigrants, so disliked as neighbours by his Conservative opponent, had been able to settle in the UK. I was dismayed by Gordon Walker's answer. He looked disturbed and, in effect, said that it wasn't his fault. I don't believe his intention was to be racist. Nowadays we'd call it 'unconscious bias,' and in the sixties most people in the UK had it in spades. One thing is certain: Gordon Walker was not the right candidate to fight a racist campaign.

I also recognised that Gordon Walker treated Atam differently from me. He welcomed him and shook his hand, but constantly ignored me and never once shook my hand or looked me in the eye.

It was much later that I understood the roots of Gordon Walker's problem. It was on Patrick Gordon Walker's watch as Commonwealth Secretary that President Seretse Khama was exiled from his country (then known as Bechuanaland, which became known after independence as Botswana). When I watched *A United Kingdom*, the film about Seretse Khama and his white English wife, Ruth Williams, I knew they had portrayed it well when government representatives treated him with respect but ignored Ruth.

I didn't know that history until the 1990 book, *A Marriage of Inconvenience* by Michael Dutfield. He described how Gordon Walker drew up a memorandum for the Cabinet, which excluded Seretse from his homeland because of his audacity in marrying a white woman.

In her brilliant book, *Colour Bar–The True Story of a Love that Shook an Empire*, Susan Williams recounts Seretse's impression of Gordon Walker and it echoed my sense of him.

'All the talk of British justice sounded empty and hollow in my ears. Exiled for five years! I simply couldn't believe it. The Secretary of State's calm and unemotional manner was unfeeling... I doubt that any man has ever been asked to give up his birthright in such cold calculating tones.'

I was full of admiration for Ruth. She was hated by racists even more than her husband was. I doubt I had her courage. Atam was right in saying that, if my parents didn't support us, life could become too tough. Thanks to Susan Williams, we know some of Ruth's perspective but that is RARE. One of the reasons why this not-exceptional woman is writing her memoir *Food of Love* is because I haven't come across significant accounts written by or about white women married to men of colour. We tend to be ignored. Racism and patriarchy cooperate in ensuring our stories are told only rarely.

The Labour Party, especially the Young Socialists, was becoming important in our social life so we invited a group of them to an engagement party at my bedsit in Handsworth. It was a 'bring a bottle' occasion. We provided snacks, which were mostly British, but introduced our friends to an Indian one, pakoras, which I had just learned how to prepare.

We brought in a supply of soft drinks. It's another example of how two people of a different culture can share a life if you are flexible. Atam is and always has been teetotal but I was developing a taste for beer. Our sons, brought up in the UK, are all social drinkers. Atam never tried to persuade us otherwise and I never urged him to drink alcohol.

My bedsit was a reasonably sized front ground-floor room but the twenty guests spilled out into the hall and front garden. At one point I found myself sitting on a stair next to a Young Socialists committee member. I tried to take what he said as a joke but it made me feel uncomfortable. I can't remember his exact words but the meaning conveyed was that I was a good-looking girl and he'd happily go out with me, that I could do better than Atam. Subtext: better than a man of colour. I didn't sleep well that night. It was as if Atam and I were the only ones actually celebrating.

I was in my final term at Smethwick Hall Secondary Modern School for girls when I was summoned to see the headmistress. The girls I'd been teaching were making good progress, better than the boys because the girls had spent most of the day in an ordinary classroom with English speakers. What could be wrong?

It turned out that conversations in the staff room were reported to her and she had taken offence over a discussion I had with a visiting teacher from the USA. We'd talked about the Empire and '*the Winds of Change*' speech by Harold Macmillan in Cape Town in 1960. In 1957, Ghana had been the first African colony to be 'given' independence. I must have said something about witnessing the end of the Empire, sounding pleased. The headmistress wanted to make it clear that she did not approve of my attitude to the British Empire. The lesson I took away was not to change my opinion but to realise how people who have a little authority try to keep control by having spies report back to them.

The girls seemed to be sorry to say goodbye to me. Just before I left, one approached me. She told me that her parents were arranging a marriage for her and she wasn't sure what to do. Given the headmistress, I had no one I could discuss it with. I was only eighteen and the responsibility felt heavy. In the situation that I saw around me, a fifteen-year-old Indian girl would be in a distressing situation if she broke from her family. There would be no support for her. I still don't know if I gave the right advice. I suggested she ask her parents to let her continue her education for at least a year so that she could take O levels. If they agreed, when the time came, she should ask that she at least meet the boy and give her approval. I learned later that she sat a few O Levels and the marriage was a success, whatever that is. But it could have been otherwise.

By October 1964 I was a student at Westminster College and Atam was teaching at George Dixon Grammar school. Atam had saved £300 deposit to buy a house and moved into 174 Putney Road, Handsworth (price £2,200). He let two rooms to a couple called Mr and Mrs Finney, hoping they would help cover overheads. They stayed five weeks and left without paying the rent!

We wrote to each other at least twice a week and I still have the letters. Atam had a telephone installed and there were coin-operated call boxes at college. I'd start the call and, when the money ran out, Atam would ring back. The day after my first call, he wrote, in rather beautiful handwriting compared to mine,

Dear Sil,
Thank you for your call. I think we need some time together soon. Don't you?
My precious, I want to hug you, kiss you and kiss you and kiss you ...

Atam was always to the point. He rarely wrote three sentences if one would do. So I was moved when I saw that he wrote 'kiss' so many times.

In order that we could more easily meet, he took his driving test and bought a little Austin A35 van that was always breaking down. During the summer holiday he came to Luton and Dad repaired the handbrake! My father taught him to do many repairs himself but it was time consuming. Atam wrote to me in September before I headed for Oxford, saying that he probably couldn't make it to Luton as the petrol would cost £1. He was short of money and had just received a big gas bill. To give a context, my teaching salary in 1967 was approximately £12 a week, so just over £600 a year. The bottom line: we tried to meet on alternate weekends.

I could not have gone to college without a government grant to cover the cost of living. I had no savings at all. There were no tuition fees but the grant was means tested. Mum and Dad were meant to give me £60 per annum but I never asked for it. The board and lodging at

Westminster was free and I was given £40 towards books, stationery and travel expenses. I needed to work during the holidays to cover personal expenses and started to work as an orderly at Luton and Dunstable Hospital in the Easter and summer holidays.

Macmillan called for a general election on 15 October 1964 and at college we held a mock election. We still weren't old enough to vote for real. I had joined the Socialist Society and became the secretary. Despite living in Handsworth and teaching in Birmingham, Atam continued to help Patrick Gordon Walker in Smethwick in the run up to the election. I may have been out of step with the prevailing culture at Westminster College, which was Liberal, but it was out of sync with the rest of the country because Labour won but with a majority of only six. It should have been eight but Labour lost two West Midlands' seats and the biggest blow was Smethwick. Conservative Peter Griffiths took the seat from Labour. After the vote count, the Conservative supporters had screamed at Patrick Gordon Walker, 'Where are your niggers now, Walker?' and 'Take your niggers away!'

After the election, Harold Wilson did something unprecedented. He made a speech attacking a new MP—and that MP was Peter Griffiths. The parliamentary correspondent, Preston Witts, wrote about Harold Wilson,

> He had a knack of making statements containing phrases that have lived on well beyond his own time, such as the "parliamentary leper" (his description of the Conservative MP who won Smethwick from Labour in 1964 after an allegedly racist campaign).

On 4 November 1964, Atam wrote to me from 174 Putney Road.

> I liked Mr Wilson's remarks about Griffiths. He's great. Who would think of a leper! He has for once finished Griffiths and this wretched creature will never be able to rise in the Tory Party. Darling, I do love you so much. I hope you are doing well at school practice.

There was a momentous event on 12 February 1965. Malcolm X visited Smethwick because the 1964 election was labelled 'the most racist election campaign in British history'. Malcolm X said that he wanted to see how Birmingham, England compared with Birmingham, Alabama. He was followed by the press but little was reported. Nine days later, Malcom X was assassinated in New York. He'd understood the significance of Marshall Street in the 'if you want a nigger for a neighbour' campaign and was photographed there. It was to be a long time and a different Smethwick, renamed Sandwell, for the town to commission a blue plaque to commemorate his visit. It is appropriately in Marshall Street.

Harold Wilson was a skilful politician. He knew the electorate wouldn't want another election straight away, in 1964, but it was hard getting through legislation with such a slim majority. There was an occasion when an MP was wheeled in on a hospital bed to vote. In March 1966, Labour won the election Wilson had called, this time with the second largest majority in its history. The Conservative leader, Edward Heath, could not compete with Wilson's popularity.

Smethwick Labour Party had to select a new candidate and boy, did it choose well. Andrew Faulds was a member of the Royal Shakespeare Company. He had been born in what was then called Tanganyika (Tanzania) to missionary parents. Andrew had not a racist bone in his body and no unconscious bias either.

Canvassing with him I immediately noticed the difference. On one occasion, Peter Griffiths and his supporters were on the opposite side of the road and Griffiths came over offering to shake Andrew's hand. With a wonderful leaning backwards, *Get Thee Behind Me Satan* sort of theatrical gesture, Andrew refused. In a pub, if anyone started racist banter Andrew would answer them forcefully—always winning the day.

February 1965: Malcolm X in Smethwick

He refused to cross the threshold of the Labour Club until the colour bar was removed. He won Smethwick back in 1966 and never lost it. Enoch Powell was the Conservative MP in nearby Wolverhampton. When he made his notorious 'rivers of blood' speech, Andrew called him, 'Unchristian, unprincipled, undemocratic and racialist.' He hadn't Wilson's ability to coin a memorable phrase but that's pretty clear language nonetheless.

Andrew asked us to invite him to our wedding. As it was held in a prefab-like church followed by a reception in wooden village hall in need of repair, I felt it wasn't going to be the kind of occasion to suit a famous actor and MP. I rather regret it now because I doubt he would have cared about the surroundings.

The new Race Relations Act came into force on 8 December 1965, which banned public displays of racism and made it illegal to discriminate on the basis of colour, race, ethnicity or nationality. With Westminster College like Utopia in comparison to Smethwick 1963/4, it felt like emerging into the light: we could put those threatening times behind us.

My recipe for Pakoras : vegetables deep-fried in a special batter.

The batter is made with chick pea flour called besan or gram flour. It's available in most supermarkets as well as South Asian shops. I vary the amount of flour according to the number I'm serving.

Method:

Sieve or spoon the flour into a deep bowl and add salt, turmeric, ground coriander, chopped fresh chilli and Amchur (mango powder if you have it)

Make a well in the flour and add one or two eggs. This is my choice; most south Asians don't add eggs. I use an electric whisk on slow and add water until the batter is creamy. Then I stir in a little natural yoghurt but that too is optional. The batter needs to be just thick enough to coat your vegetables. Once it's the right consistency I put the whisk on high to incorporate lots of air. The batter will keep for a couple of days in a fridge.

The most popular vegetable to use for pakoras is potato. (Parboil them or use sliced leftovers.) Coat uncooked sliced peppers and mushrooms and salted sliced aubergine. Optional: sprinkle chopped spinach and onions over the potatoes or add them to the batter.

To Deep Fry

Heat vegetable oil in a wok. The fat has to be hot but not smoky. Dip a slice of vegetable in the batter and put it in the sizzling fat. You can cook a few at a time. Place the cooked pakoras on greaseproof paper or kitchen towel to absorb excess fat. Serve sprinkled with salt, fresh coriander and, if you have access to an Indian shop, Chaat Masala.

CHAPTER 8: Westminster College

Education in the UK was nurtured by the churches, particularly the Anglican church. The Methodists founded Westminster College in 1851 to train men and women to become teachers. It was situated in Horseferry Road, a stone's throw from Westminster Abbey and the iconic Methodist Central Hall. It became over-subscribed so, in 1872, Southlands College for women was founded and Westminster became for men only. It developed a reputation for training teachers of the highest calibre.

After WW2 the college faced a serious problem. Situated as it was in the heart of the capital, it could not enlarge. Not only that, the buildings had been damaged during the war and major structural repairs were impossible with students in residence. The site was valuable so they decided to sell up. The Horseferry Road site is now the headquarters of Channel 4.

In 1959, Westminster College moved out of London, into a purpose-built campus set proud on Harcourt Hill on the western edge of Oxford, overlooking the dreaming spires. It was a delightful place to live with its fusion of Oxford quads and New England style architecture, and it once again admitted female students.

Following the move, the college's qualifications were validated by the University of Oxford through its Institute of Education. The BEd Oxford was approved with some reluctance by the ancient university, which never welcomed Westminster with a spirit of belonging. There was hope that it would eventually become a college of the University, but this was always refused. Eventually in 2000, the college became home to Westminster Institute of Education and part of Oxford Brookes University. The Westminster name continues but it has lost its independence.

Because the demand for teachers was increasing rapidly, the only way to accommodate everyone was for some first-years to share a room. My roommate was Angela Hughes from Bath. Her background was similar to mine: we were among the few students of working-class origin, except Angela was way ahead of me in her transition to the middle class. Her mother must have been a fan of *My Fair Lady*, because she'd encouraged her daughter to have elocution lessons and Angela had acquired quite a plummy accent. We soon teamed up with the occupant of the adjacent room, Annie Metherell. She was accustomed to meeting new people in new places because she had attended seven schools.

Westminster College 1965.
I'm second on the left in the front row between Patsy and Angela. Annie is in the back row on the right. Sixties fashion hadn't yet spread beyond the capital!

On my first Friday evening at Westminster, some of us headed down the hill to The Fishes. I wrote to Atam, 'It has a fabulous atmosphere. I only had one glass of cider so you needn't worry. I had an interesting discussion with the president of the Conservative Association.' If I were writing it today, I'd have added in a 'LOL.'

At the heart of the campus was an American-style chapel where services were held twice a day. It wasn't compulsory to attend but it was expected. My attendance was infrequent and I met another student who, like me, was not a keen chapel goer. His name was John Stone, known as Rocky. We both joined the Socialist Society but I discovered that he was a Trotskyite, whereas I'd become involved in politics to fight racism. Temperamentally I'm adverse to dogma.

In a letter to Atam I wrote, 'Rocky told me that I'm lucky to be engaged because I would be too mature for most of the men here and wouldn't stand for continual conversation about school and college, college and school. He has offered to let you kip on his floor so that means you can stay here for free.' In case you missed it, there was absolutely no way that we would be sharing a bed while I was a student.

The common room had a café but, because it was a Methodist college, alcohol wasn't allowed. The Fresher's Fair was buzzing even if only lubricated with coffee and colas. One of the activities I signed up for was the Debating Society. The Students Union organised a WUS week (World Union of Students). It was a Rag Week extravaganza when students let off steam and also raised money for scholarships for African students. Many members of the staff and students had African connections.

In November 1965, Ian Smith, prime minister of what was then called Rhodesia (Zimbabwe) made a Unilateral Declaration of Independence, the first colony to declare its independence without the approval of the British Parliament since the USA declared its independence in 1776. The news struck like an electric shock. Things were to get even worse for the Black citizens of that country as the white minority refused to be blown by the winds of change sweeping the continent.

There was a link with the college because one of the daughters of former Liberal PM, Reginald Garfield Todd, who'd opposed white minority rule, had been a student. His oldest daughter, Judith, was a courageous opponent not only of Smith, who'd imprisoned her, but she later also suffered worse under Mugabe. My awareness of segregation and the cruelty involved in the Empire was growing. The college magazine, *The Westminsterian*, reported from Old W's in Africa. They were filled with the spirit of Uhuru (Freedom). For the Hilary term 1965 magazine, I wrote a feature titled *Why Politics?* It seems relevant today.

Unless practised by a literate and intelligent populace, democracy can degenerate into oligarchy. A few ambitious people fired with hunger for power can capture the party machinery and ultimately the machinery of government.

I used Barry Goldwater, the Republican candidate, as an example. Today, someone could use Donald Trump.

During Rag Weeks, we were spoilt for choice of activities because every house and society planned something. I organised a debate and the proposal was, '*Vice is Nice and Lust is a Must.*' It was, shall we say, risqué.

Rocky and I joined the university's Labour Club. Among the speakers was Andrew Faulds, described as 'by profession an actor: Secretary of the British Committee for Peace in Vietnam: Labour Candidate for Smethwick in the next election.' Another was Ralph Miliband, the father of Ed and David.

I persuaded my friends to canvass for Labour in the working-class area of St Ebbe's in the lead up to the November 1964 election. Our candidate Evan Luard sadly lost but then won two years later in 1966. I can only guess at what those poor voters thought of these young women, who couldn't themselves vote, telling them what to do.

I chose History and English as my main subjects and I was training to teach children aged 9-13. Education, PE and Maths were compulsory. For my two minor topics, I chose art and geography. Annie and Angela had chosen the same academic subjects. And we all did drama. Each year group had to put on plays at the end of the second year. Angela and I chose to take part in a surreal production of the *Future is in Eggs* by Eugene Ionesco. You don't get more 1960s than that.

Drama became significant in Angie and Annie's lives because they worked as assistant stage managers on the University's Opera Society's production of *The Rise and Fall of the City of Mahagonny*. Given the ratio of men to women in Oxford at that time, they were welcomed and met their future husbands, Thomas Prag, who later founded Moray Firth Radio Station, and Chris Wright, who became group operations director at AEA technology in Harwell.

In the sixties, there were four Oxford colleges for women and all the others were for men only. The prevailing attitude towards women was evident. In the early seventies, Princetown University Professor Leon Kamin visited Atam and I when he was investigating Cyril Burt— the fraudulent proposer of the tripartite system of education. Leon told us about his first visit to Oxford and his embarrassment when he realised that his wife wasn't included in the invitation to stay in college.

Most of us can remember one teacher who helped change our lives. My history tutor, Donald Tranter, was to have a profound influence on me. He taught us modern history and his choice of curriculum was radical for the time. For two terms the subject was the history of modern China. It was an extraordinary Chinese history syllabus and Donald brought it up to the then present day. Without that foundation I doubt I'd have been able to write *Brushstrokes in Time*, which is mostly set in China.

Many years later, when Donald became a customer of mine at the Jam Factory, he joked that I was one of the PITS: the Pool of Inactive Teachers!

In 2009, I interviewed Dame Jessica Rawson, who was one of THE THREE, that is, one the first three women to become heads of an old Oxford College, in her case Merton in 1994. I could empathise with her. Like me, she had been interested in India and China from a young age. She'd been head girl at a famous school but said, 'I suppose I was bright but I was lonely.' She wanted to study Chinese history and Mandarin but her head teacher said, 'No one goes to China, no one learns Chinese history, no one learns Mandarin.' She was bullied into applying to study European history at Cambridge, and it was a hard struggle for Jessica to eventually follow her dream.

Compared with most modern-day courses we had an intense pro- gramme of lectures, seminars and tutorials, which we were expected to attend, and were given lots of assignments. I wrote to Atam,

Today I had seven lectures and was given three essays and one Maths class observation report to write. This is my half hour free before dinner, after which I must get stuck into, 'When and Why did the American Policy of Isolation End?'

For an English essay, *A Critical Appreciation of September 1913 by WB Yeats,* I got an 'A+' and it established my love of the poet. That was why I chose the Irish poet for the subject of my final thesis. I joined the Poetry Circle and my letters to Atam were filled with poems by Donne, Shakespeare, Cecil Day Lewis and me! My poetry oozed with intensity and sentiment, with titles like *Beyond Reason* and *Living Death.* The ones I am not too embarrassed to share were either comic or simple.

An Epitaph

He was forced to leave Delhi
For conspiracies many,
And to this fair isle
He came with a smile,
And dallied a while
With a maid without guile
Till enamoured was she
And Labour would be
But they looked to the Left
And forgot to look Right
And this lack of surveyance
A Tory conveyance
Decided their end
On the Orpington Bend.

The reference was to the famous Orpington by election in 1962 which signalled that support was slipping away from the Conservative Government. It was won, not by Labour but by the Liberals.

Question and Answer

Is love glad?
Why Yes
Then it isn't sad?
But it is.
Love is giving
and receiving.
Illogical
Paradoxical
Nonsensical
But none the less wonderful.

I wrote to Atam at speed to catch the post and my longhand was not the most legible so I sometimes treated him and borrowed a friend's typewriter. The to-ing and fro-ing to the post box was noticed. Patsy gave Angela and me a Christmas present of a letter rack: 'Because you get so much mail.'

In addition to the academic work, we had teaching practice. I wrote to Atam after my first day at Freeland,

> *'The Headmistress rather resents my presence. She only wanted one student and was pressed to take two, the second being me. There really isn't room for three teachers.'*

Freeland is a small village near Witney and the school only had two classes. The head teacher took the junior class of children aged 7-11 and her daughter taught the infant class. The lecturer who inspected me, Dr Laws, gave me a good report. I kept a few copies of the children's poetry writing and it was pretty good. We had to write a self-criticism after each lesson. To give readers who have had more recent experience of teaching, I'll share one:

The children were enthusiastic and I commended their writing and drawing. Unfortunately the poetry reading was spoilt by the noise of the digger outside, a dog barking, and the church bell ringing (next door).

As good as it was, my next teaching practice at Charlbury school was even better.

The class was aged 9-10. It was idyllic. I was allowed to take the children ponding and on field studies. Nearby was a surviving corner of a wildflower meadow of kaleidoscopic beauty. We collected flowers to press, mount and label. I gave them copies of Rupert Brooke's, *These I Have Loved* and taught them a few techniques like onomatopoeia and alliteration and encouraged them to write their own 'These I Have Loved' poems. We put on a play with an audience of two lower junior classes and I taught them fractions.

I certainly didn't take the advice of Dr Oxley, my tutor. The bluff Yorkshire man was fond of saying, 'A word and a blow and a blow first'. He said his first teaching experience was in the East End of London. Although corporal punishment in school and at home was not unusual in those times, I never hit a child.

Three meals were provided in the Westminster canteen and were similar to my old school dinners. The food I remember most was what we prepared ourselves in the house kitchen. Each week we collected a tea box which contained sliced bread, butter and jam, marmite, tea and coffee. Around 4:30, we gathered in the kitchen to make tea and toast and chat. Another example of *communessence*? What is it about eating together that makes you feel together?

During WUS week, I had my first taste of homemade Chinese food. A student in another house sold Egg Fu Yung (for the student charity). I wasn't alone at Westminster being in a mixed relationship. She was engaged to a guy of Chinese ancestry. I expect their reasons for being engaged were similar to Atam and mine, and our attempt to ward off judgements, given that white women who were seen with men of colour were regarded as immoral. We had our twenty-first, key-of-the-door birthdays while students and one of the nicest Chinese meals I ate in a decade was in a restaurant in Little Clarendon Street where Annie chose to celebrate her birthday.

You would think that with all the good food, I'd have put on weight. I was skinny when I arrived, weighing just 7 stone 4 lb (46 kilos). When the nurse discovered that I'd lost weight and was only 6 stone 10 lbs, she wanted me to see the doctor. He prescribed a glass of milk and a banana with every meal. I was not anorexic. I enjoyed my food but I burnt it off quickly as life was full. My whole life has been about juggling balls. When I was young, that kept me thin. It doesn't anymore. And that's fine with me too.

Rocky Stone was probably right about the three of us having more experience of the world than many of our age group. A mature student called Tim seemed attracted to us. Tim had managed a rubber plantation in Malaysia. He married a much younger woman who didn't enjoy their social life relying on a small group of expats. She entertained herself with affairs which led to them coming back to England and Tim filing for a divorce. He was bitter and cynical about it but we sensed something beneath his hard shell. Annie had been brought up in Singapore and, because she had an empathetic ear, he enjoyed talking to her in particular about his life in the Malaysian jungle.

On a history trip to London, Tim persuaded Angela and me to go with him to the Old Bailey to sit in a divorce court. In those days you had to prove guilt in order to get a divorce. Desertion, non-consummation or adultery had to be proved. I suspect Tim was getting prepared but it was sad to watch the human misery on display. Then he took us to Bow Street Magistrates court. We walked in and stood at the back. It was a cold February day and Angie and I were wearing our college scarfs. A young police sergeant was in the witness box giving evidence about a strip club. The judge asked him, 'So what was this young womandoing?'

'She was rubbing a feather boa between her legs,' was the reply. Next to me, Angie guffawed. The judge glared daggers at us and took in our college scarfs. We left in a hurry. Like my brother's experience when gambling was illegal, that court case and those divorce trials wouldn't happen now.

On a Saturday in February another mate, Carole, took me to her home in Trowle Common, Trowbridge in Wiltshire for a long weekend. This was my first experience of staying in a middle-class home (apart from with Brigitte in Germany). Carole had her own car and drove us to her modern, elegant, detached home with a detached garage set in a large garden with a paddock behind. They had a telephone and it was centrally heated. Despite that, I felt cold and wore thick woolly jumpers because the thermostat was not set high. It was just me who felt that way, probably because of my weight loss. Carole's parents were kind, sincere, religious people so we attended church twice on Sunday. The next day we went to sightsee in Bath before returning to Oxford.

During the Easter holidays a few weeks later, I took a trip to Sarisbury Green to stay in the attractive four-bedroomed modern house that my brother Ray had built! Whether through friendships or education or hard work, we were moving up and into the middle class.

Annie's father was a Methodist minister so moved around a lot but had been sent to the county of our shared ancestry, Cornwall. That summer they invited us to stay in the manse (the Methodist equivalent of the Vicarage) in Newquay. Atam and I drove to Bath to collect Angie and then set off for Cornwall. There were no motorways in those days. Driving down a steep hill on a bend, the van turned over. Luckily none of us were hurt apart from the odd bump and bruise. The RAC came to our rescue and we made it to Cornwall. We enjoyed the then not-crowded Newquay beaches and I saw surfing for the first time. The sport had recently been introduced to Cornwall by four Aussie lifeguards.

The rest of the summer I needed to work and earn some money, so I returned to Luton and Dunstable hospital and my job as an orderly cleaning a ward, delivering meals and making egg sandwiches for the patients' afternoon tea. But I was obsessed with learning to drive and Dad started teaching me on his newly acquired Vauxhall Viva.

In my second year at Westminster, Atam worried that I was moving away from him. I replied to one letter, *'It's not flattering. I like to think you love ME and not just a sense of belonging'*. In January 1966, we decided to end our frustration and get married that summer. I could complete my qualification as a married student as 'mature' students were no longer odd beings. Needless to say my college friends were invited to our wedding in 1966. The Principal was supportive and even sent us a wedding present.

The artist, Weimin He appears later in my story. His version of:

Egg Fou Yung: Chinese Scrambled eggs and tomato

(notice the importance of COLOUR!)

Ingredients

> 3 medium tomatoes
> 1-2 spring onions
> 3 eggs
> 1/2 teaspoon salt
> 2-3 tablespoon light soy sauce
> One tablespoon sesame oil
> One teaspoon shaoxing wine (optional)
> One teaspoon shanxi vinegar
> One or two tablespoons vegetable oil
> 1/2 teaspoon sugar (optional) and coriander

Method

Start by chopping 2-3 medium size tomatoes into small wedges.

Finely chop 2 spring onions. Then crack 2-3 eggs into a bowl and season with 1 teaspoon shanxi vinegar, and 1 teaspoon Shaoxing wine (optional). Beat eggs for 30 seconds.

Preheat the wok with medium fire for 30 seconds, then add 1-2 tablespoons of vegetable oil, and add the eggs. Scramble the eggs and remove from the wok when the eggs are 85% cooked (important, do not get the eggs thoroughly cooked). Set the scramble aside.

Add 1 more tablespoon oil to the wok, turn up the heat to high, and add the tomatoes, spring onions and some black pepper.

Stir-fry for 1 minute, then add 1/2 teaspoon sugar, 1/2 teaspoon salt (or to taste), and 1-2 tablespoons of light soy sauce, add a few tablespoon of water. After boiling, when the tomato are completely softened, add the scramble, mix everything together, then add a few drops of sesame oil, then put into a dish. Chop a few pieces of coriander put on top of the dish as well as more fresh spring onions, you will see the red, yellow and green colours. Serve with steamed plain rice (ideally sushi rice).

CHAPTER 9: Mrs Sylvia Vetta

On July 9 1966, I became Mrs Vetta. Atam's most appreciated gift to me was his name. Dad joked that 'Harry' was the name for the devil. Atam's caste name was Sachdeva but he didn't believe in caste (which works much like racism) and so adopted the Sanskrit name. The most appreciated present I gave him was an exquisitely illustrated copy of Nagsh-e Chagtai published in Lahore in 1946, which I found in an antiquarian bookshop. Even now, Atam loves to quote Ghalib couplets but the culture from his childhood when he learned to love the Urdu poet has vanished. The Saudi version of Islam has upstaged Sufi Islam in Pakistan and Wahhabists wouldn't approve of his sensual verse, and if Ghalib were alive today, some crazy guy would probably end up killing him.

July 1966 : Our wedding in Luton

We married in Round Green Methodist Church, which has long since been demolished, not by hate but by the advancement of the consumer society. Atam stayed the night before with my Auntie Ada in Letchworth, and they made sure he arrived on time. He had no problem with the Christian ceremony. The choir came for free to sing Love Divine. My Uncle Leslie, the Salvation Army officer, was allowed to perform the ceremony with the minister. Auntie Alice did the scripture reading.

There was no way that any of Atam's family could afford to come to England. Atam's friends from Nuneaton and Graham Newis would have looked a bit sad on their own so we asked everyone to spread out on both sides of the chapel. Our guests were Mum's family, Jean's family (my sister-in-law), Luton friends and neighbours, and my new friends from Westminster College. Surprise, surprise, none of Dad's close relations from Cornwall made the effort to attend or send a card or telegram. But his second cousins from Sennen, the lovely Hilda and Herbert, sent a card and a present and apologies because it was the height of the B&B season.

The reception was in a wooden village hall five miles from Luton. The church hall was better but, because Methodists don't allow alcohol on the premises, Dad thought it wouldn't be popular with our guests. Teetotaller Atam paid for champagne, and there was a bar and a sit-down meal followed by the cutting of the cake, made by Aunt Eva. Then the big secret surprise: Dad asked Atam and I to go with him outside. He led us to the red telephone box and it rang.

'Pick it up,' said Dad.

'Hello,' said a familiar voice with only a trace of an Australian accent. I burst into tears.

It had taken effort and money to arrange the four-minute call from Sydney. I made sure Michael spoke to Mum, as well as introducing him to his new brother–in–law. There were more tears following that than in the church.

Atam booked a special honeymoon by the standards of 1966. Thomas Cook was the first company to organise foreign holidays in 1855, but cheap package holidays combining flight, transfers and accommodation only started to take off in the sixties. Four days after our wedding, we flew from Birmingham airport to Berne in Switzerland and then travelled by coach through the Alps into Italy and to Liguria and the resort of Diano Marina near Genoa. It felt wildly exotic to this working-class girl.

I revelled in the sun, sand and warm sea. I was used to holding my breath while wading into the cold Atlantic, and had never used sun block, as it was a rare commodity then. When I suffered a day of prickly heat, the sunscreen the pharmacy recommended was expensive, but I had no option but to buy it. The final day, 30 July was special. The TV in the lounge/bar televised the World Cup Final from Wembley and the English guests celebrated long and hard. Emerging bleary-eyed at breakfast the next day, many looked unprepared for the journey home. The waiters smiled at them still swaying and saying, 'We won the Cup.' All good humoured. I was happy beyond words.

∞

Back in Handsworth, I set about getting to know our neighbours. On our left was a middle-class widow. Mrs Pritchard's son was an artist, primarily a print maker. She introduced me to antiques, especially her collection of Chinese tea bowls and early English porcelain. On our right were a retired working-class couple, Mr and Mrs Wilkins. They were helpful neighbours but Mrs Wilkins taught me that prejudice is completely irrational. One day she stopped me on the street to complain that something had to be done about the immigrants. They were all on National Assistance (NA)—the name for benefits in 1966.

I replied, 'Atam's an immigrant but he's not on National Assistance.'

'Atam isn't an immigrant,' replied Mrs W.

Her other neighbour, Mr King, was originally from the West Indies. He'd helped with her garden when Mr Wilkins was ill. 'The Kings are not on NA,' I said.

Apparently, the Kings were not immigrants either.

She had recently attended the wedding of the daughter of another Jamaican couple, the Davis's. They too were not immigrants. The couple opposite were Bill and Minette Morris. She was a nurse and he worked in the car industry.

'The Morris's are not on NA.'

No, they weren't immigrants.

'So who are the immigrants?' I asked Mrs Wilkins.

A black couple further up the road qualified. He had just been laid off from the Austin/Morris car factory.

Bill Morris had joined the Transport and General Workers' Union in 1958, and had recently become a shop steward. He complained to Atam about prevailing racist attitudes within the Trade Union Movement. Atam suggested the best way was for him to try to get elected onto the National Executive in order to change things. He did so and famously became General Secretary. A few months before he sat his eleven plus, I gave their eldest son a bit of free tuition.

Recipe: Our sixties wedding starter: Prawn Cocktail

Ingredients

400g cooked Atlantic shell-on prawns

2 little gem or one iceberg lettuce

3 heaped tbsp mayonnaise

(Mayonnaise was popular in the sixties /seventies. Nowadays I replace it with yoghurt)

4 tbsp tomato chutney

2 tsp Worcester sauce

tsp horseradish

Splash of Tabasco sauce

Squeeze of lemon juice

Paprika, for dusting

Optional chopped chives, parsley or coriander garnish

Method

Peel the prawns.

Break the lettuce into individual leaves and divide the leaves between four small glass bowls. Put the prawns on the lettuce and season with black pepper. Retain a few for garnish.

Mix the mayonnaise, chutney, Worcestershire sauce, horseradish and Tabasco together. Season to taste with lemon juice and salt and pepper.

Combine with the prawns just before serving.

Spoon over the prawns.

Dust the top with a little paprika and sprinkle with chives. Top with the remaining prawns and serve immediately.

CHAPTER 10: Teaching Myself.

I applied to teach at St Mary's Church of England Junior school in Hamstead Road, a ten-minute walk from our house. A new school had been built but they couldn't close the Victorian building situated in a neighbouring street because the school population had grown so rapidly. The C19th building consisted of four small classrooms with sliding dividers. I was allocated two of them for my class of seven-year olds, all forty of them! Half the class was black and half white.

I was faced with a challenging situation. Eight had not started school until they were six due to lack of space, even though that was illegal. Given that many were children of immigrants, their parents had not complained. So reading ability ranged from zero to good. I was given a teaching assistant every morning and I don't know how I'd have coped without her. She forgave me for making her concentrate on teaching the children who couldn't, to read.

Inspired by Charlbury, we sometimes took the class into the play-ground for practical maths, mapping the area, bug hunting and collecting leaves in nearby Handsworth Park for use in nature studies and art. I believe that activity helps boys, in particular, to concentrate.

There was no National Curriculum in 1967. The textbooks available were old and uninspiring. The headmistress worked hard to change that and helped me to create a reading corner with more engaging books. It fell far below my library dreams but it was a start. At college I'd visited some progressive schools using a cutting-edge new pedagogy, child-centred education; that is, children to a certain extent could direct their own learning. For that approach to be successful, small classes, individual monitoring and strict record keeping are essential. I'd no idea how to achieve that with such a diverse class of forty pupils. I decided to have a formal classroom at one end and an informal one at the other. First thing in the morning I sat the children in rows like my classroom at Hart Hill Junior. Each row was a team and each pupil could earn points for completing their work. At the end of the week I'd give the winning team sweets. The children could do more exciting work in the informal end once they had finished their individual 3Rs assignments.

It was my probationary year and when the inspector came, I was teaching at the formal end of the classroom. One boy started to play up. I asked him by name to settle down but I got the impression that the inspector thought I should have been stricter. Remember corporal punishment was the norm in large classes. Fortunately I did pass.

Annie and Angela were having an even tougher time. Annie was teaching in Small Heath, an area of high deprivation, and had a class of 47-50 children with no assistant. Many of the parents suffered from alcohol abuse and their children arrived at school hungry. In November 1966, a docu-drama called *Cathy Come Home*, directed by Ken Loach and set in a similar district, shone a light on homelessness and dire poverty. Anyone who thinks the sixties was all love and miniskirts, the Beatles and surfing, should watch it.

Annie went on to teach at Manchester's Trafford Language Centre in the early seventies. It was like a hub: non-English-speaking children from primary schools attended in the morning and secondary pupils in the afternoon. I gave her my copy of English for New Australians, and she adapted it herself using terraced houses labelled 'Mr and Mrs Patel live here'. They were given donations of books. When she trawled through them, she ended up rejecting most in which a black or brown person was portrayed because they were racist. She went to Bradford, where a group were producing material in which some ethnic minority people were represented. She also attempted to cull the books patronising to women but gave up on that one. She couldn't get rid of all of them or they would have had a pitiful collection. In those days, John did all the active things while Janet looked on, and the leaders were always boys.

Sharing notes, we realised that our education at Westminster had been primarily academic and we had to learn on the job. In 1964 Sir John Maude was appointed to lead a Royal Commission on Local Government. The principal asked him to visit our college in our first year to inspire us in our vocation. Maude's mantra was, *'The best way to learn is to teach.'* But I felt I needed to learn *how* to teach.

∞

I'd love to tell you that Atam and I had time for fun but I'd be lying. In 1967, Aston University advertised a MSc course in Statistics and Operational Research. Wednesbury College arranged his teaching timetable for afternoons and evenings to enable him to attend the morning classes at Aston University. Atam ate at college, and I relied on school dinners for the main meal of my day. I worked in the evening on marking and preparation, watched TV including the news for one hour and went to bed soon after he returned home at ten, exhausted. I'd always been an avid reader but that year I read not one book for pleasure until the summer holidays when I treated myself to the Lord of the Rings trilogy.

I signed up for a weekend coach trip to London, for Birmingham teachers to see *Fiddler on the Roof,* which had opened with rave reviews. Atam had to do course work and preparation at the weekends and couldn't come with me.

The musical is set in early C20th Russia at a time of Czarist pogroms against the Jews. Tevye is a milkman who tries to maintain his Jewish culture in the face of powerful antisemitism. It ends with the Czar evicting Jews from the village. In the audience were some kinder-transport children and their children, and the powerful emotion that it tapped into was of grief.

Given the musical we had just witnessed, you will comprehend the shock I felt at an incident on the journey home. I was seated on the front seat of the coach next to a young Welsh teacher. From time to time the coach driver joined in our conversation and appeared to have a good sense of humour. I must have mentioned Atam's new post to my companion. The driver turned jokingly, 'So you're Eve to his Adam?'

'No,' I replied. 'His name is Atam,' emphasising the T.

He asked the origin of the name. I explained that it was Sanskrit. He hadn't heard of Sanskrit. When I explained, his mood changed. 'He's an Indian?' When I replied in the affirmative, angry abuse rained down including, 'He should be strung up.'

I felt battered. The shock meant that I didn't immediately respond. At last I said, 'I assume you are supporter of the National Front.' He said he wasn't a member but hatred of immigrants poured out. I looked towards my companion, hoping she'd support me. Instead, she added to my discomfort by saying that her husband felt there should be the death penalty for a coloured man raping a white woman.

When Atam and I became engaged I knew we would meet preju-dice, but witnessing Andrew Faulds win back Smethwick and the soli-darity of Westminster College with the Winds of Change in Africa and support for the Civil Rights Movement, I had felt optimism. On the rest of that journey back to Birmingham I felt fear.

There was as well a kind of despair. If a teacher from Wales who had just seen a powerful piece about systemic discrimination could not support me, then really, what would it take?

The horror and fear did not stop there. On 20 April, 1968, Enoch Powell, using scare stories to demonise the minorities, delivered what became known as 'the rivers of blood speech'.

Powell's finale hit the headlines and 'the rivers of blood speech' injected toxic pollution into the political psyche. It was Smethwick all over again, but this time writ large. For those who don't know it, I have copied it below:

For these dangerous and divisive elements (immigrants, in particular the Sikhs), the legislation proposed in the Race Relations Bill is the very pabulum they need to flourish. Here is the means of showing that the immigrant communities can organise to consolidate their members, to agitate and campaign against their fellow citizens, and to overawe and dominate the rest with the legal weapons which the ignorant and the ill-informed have provided. As I look ahead, I am filled with foreboding; like the Roman, I seem to see "the River Tiber foaming with much blood."

Within two days that speech affected my class. The children had previously played together in a colour-blind manner. Their innocence was lost, presumably because of what parents said to them, comments on the street and newspaper headlines. I walked into the playground to see the white children at one end and the black at the other.

I'd been contemplating casting my vote, not for Labour, but for a Conservative. The irony of it! The sitting MP, Edward Boyle, gave his name to the 1945 Education Act. He was from Eton and Christ Church-educated landed gentry—not an obvious choice to represent me. In comparison, the Labour candidate for Handsworth was a decent man but lacked intelligence, charisma, energy and the ability to organise in multi-racial Handsworth. In Smethwick, I'd learned that the individual candidate matters.

Enoch Powell was the MP for Smethwick's neighbour, Wolver-hampton, and the pressure was on the liberal-minded Boyle to support him. He refused. Like Edward Heath, he did what he could to counter his malign influence. In 1970, Boyle resigned. He didn't say why but it was obvious: he had lost the support of his Powell-supporting local party. My dilemma was lifted but it wasn't good news.

Decades later I interviewed the director of the Pegasus Youth Theatre in Oxford. In 1965, Jamaican-born Euton Daley arrived in Birmingham to live with his parents in a two-up two-down house in nearby Aston. Euton was fortunate because he had a drama teacher called Laurie Walsh who believed in him and encouraged him. As I have always maintained, teachers can make a substantial difference in people's lives, and are agents of change. Sadly, that was not always the case. In my annexe, the other teacher hated having to teach 'niggers'. She emigrated to Australia with its whites-only immigration policy. She was an exception at St Mary's but low expectations of working class and minority children has been and still is a blight on our education system.

This Caribbean recipe that reflected my Handsworth neighbours' cuisine was given to me by the founder of the Cowley Road Soup Kitchen, Icolyn Smith, who grew up in rural Jamaica and was the inspiration for a character named after her in my book co-written with Nancy Mudenyo Hunt, *Not So Black and White*.

Icolyn's Jerk Chicken

Ingredients

1kg chicken
2 tablespoon jerk seasoning
1medium onion
2 cloves garlic
1 teaspoon black pepper

Method

Wash chicken with lemon.
Place in an ovenproof dish.
Chop onion and garlic add to chicken.
Stir together with all the other ingredients.
Cover with cling film and leave it in the fridge overnight.
Put in oven and cook until chicken is tender.

CHAPTER 11: Justin

It is a measure of how the world had already changed that we cared deeply and knew a lot about the Vietnam War. After the assassination of John F Kennedy his successor, Lyndon Johnson, was more interested in civil rights and domestic issues, and left Vietnam to the generals, who escalated the conflict until there was a presence of nearly 400,000 U.S. troops in Vietnam by the end of 1966. The emotional trigger for worldwide protests was the My Lai Massacre, in which frustrated US soldiers killed hundreds of unarmed Vietnamese civilians in a small village. Protests against the war broke out in dozens of American cities. Here we were, citizens of one country protesting another country's actions in a third country. It was not just the movement of people and goods that was going global, so had popular pushback.

I was young and idealistic and critical of Harold Wilson for not con-demning the war. With the wisdom of age, when I compare Wilson to Blair and Iraq, I realise Harold was a genius. He kept British troops out of the war while not alienating the USA.

Atam and I joined the Birmingham Committee for Peace in Vietnam. We sent coaches to Red Lion Square in March to join the protests in front of the US embassy but we also marched and spread information in Birmingham. One Saturday morning in June 1968, I had a phone call.

'We have a loudspeaker van available. Can you help?'

The driver was a young man called Dave and I was in charge of the mike. He drove around the shopping streets while I talked about stopping the war. He joked that I sounded like the Queen. But the humour ceased when a police car flagged us down. We had to follow it to the central police station. Dave became increasingly agitated. I asked what was wrong. He'd protested against Polaris nuclear submarines based at Faslane, and been arrested and beaten up by the police. I tried to reassure him.

'Look,' I said, 'leave this one to me. They're not going to beat up a pregnant woman.'

When we arrived, I suggested Dave stay seated on the bench while I go to the desk. The committee hadn't notified the police—it had all been naively spur of the moment. I apologised and promised we wouldn't do it again without a licence. In 1968's patriarchal society, there were occasions when it was advantageous being a woman.

Atam and I were rather shaken when I missed a period immediately after we stopped taking precautions. The delight quickly turned to anxiety when I was told that there were cases of German Measles or Rubella at St Mary's. Rubella doesn't make you feel ill but it is dangerous to an embryo and can cause deafness, blindness and/or a hole in heart. In 1968, there was no vaccination against the disease. I couldn't be certain that I was pregnant because you couldn't buy tests in pharmacies then. I trotted off to the GP, who confirmed that I was having a baby. I told him about the Rubella outbreak and thought he would prescribe sick leave. He declined but said he would give me an injection of Gamma Globulin which should protect me. It didn't.

I was just over nine weeks pregnant when I caught Rubella. What should have been a joyful time in our lives became a nightmare. Our child would be cherished but as a mixed-race child, if disabled by the Rubella, what would his future be? I struggled hard to control my feelings.

I was booked into the newly built Queen Elizabeth hospital. I went into labour and after six hours we made our way to the hospital. Twenty-seven hours later I was exhausted but finally ready to go the delivery room. It was unusual then for the husband to attend the birth but it was agreed that Atam could come with me.

He was gowned up and, after the porter had wheeled me in and shut the door, we were alone. Ten minutes later a midwife put her head around the door, saw a brown man in a gown and assuming Atam was a doctor, said, 'Okay, you're all right,' and left before we could reply.

I'd never seen Atam look so pale!

I hadn't met the midwife who eventually helped us. She was a large woman of West Indian ancestry. She seemed experienced but was not empathetic and was rough compared to the midwives I was to enjoy in the John Radcliffe for my next two deliveries. The cord was tangled tightly around Justin's neck, she cut me quickly and brutally without telling me what she was about to do. I changed GP just before the birth and he was shocked when he later saw the damage.

When Justin emerged, he didn't cry. It is hard to describe our emotion when at last, we heard his little voice. Because of the trauma he was placed in an incubator and whisked away. The elation I felt being able to hold my next two sons, Adrian and Paul, when they were born was not possible, and I floundered beneath a cloud of fear and depression.

Eventually they let me see him. He was perfect. When I nestled him in my arms, I experienced relief tinged with serene delirium. On the fourth day he was allowed on the ward and I was able to feed him. On day six he had a visitor: the Queen Mother opened the hospital. Our picture appeared in the Birmingham Post.

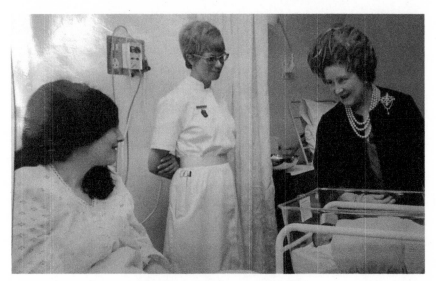

The Queen Mother meets Justin

The indications were that Justin was not harmed by the Rubella. But when he was two, I was worried that he wasn't talking enough and tests revealed that he was deaf in one ear. At first they thought the cause was fluid behind the ear and operated a couple of times. More sophisticated tests when he was eleven revealed damage to the middle ear that had indeed been caused by the Rubella. By then he was doing well at school and so we generally ignored it and treated Justin as if there was nothing wrong.

Possibly that approach was also because there were times when I found motherhood overwhelming. I didn't know then that being over-whelmed is a relatively common occurrence for mothers. I muscled through it, dropping balls and occasionally treating problems as if they weren't ones. I should probably take this opportunity to apologise to my children. I just didn't know how else to be.

Atam had passed his MSc so his working hours were more regular but he'd joined the lecturers' union National Association of Teachers in Further and Higher Education (NATFHE). When Justin was three months old, about 9.30 pm one evening in March, Atam was late back after a union meeting. I heard screams coming from the street and ran to the door. The woman was clearly in distress, shouting at someone and looking afraid.

I asked if she would like to come inside and she did. I sat her on the sofa and asked if I could get her tea or coffee. She calmed down. She was a prostitute, fleeing from a difficult client. After a while she felt it was safe to leave, thanked me, went out into the dark street and I never saw her again.

I hadn't seen the man she was running from. Maybe it was he who pushed the unsigned letter without an envelope through our door. The writing was jumbled, like you'd expect from an anonymous threat. It was mostly racist garbage but also associated me with prostitutes. *Niggers and nigger lovers should get out.*

Powell had campaigned for repatriation, and that is what the fascists wanted. Any black or brown face was anathema to them. When a few weeks later another came through the door. I didn't read it. The torn pieces went straight into the bin. I resolved not to be upset: that way the racists would not win. The more Justin interacted with me and was able to play, the more I loved him, and the more I took pleasure in being a mother. So that day, I took him in the pushchair to the park to feed the ducks and resolved not to tell Atam about the second letter. Maybe the strategy worked because there were no more.

I insisted on being resilient. It wasn't an option. I was determined my son would have a happy childhood whatever the obstacles put in our way.

But there may have been a downside to needing to be strong. I forgot how to show vulnerability, or be vulnerable at any level. Now that I am old, I can say that there is no perfect way to deal with entrenched racism and hostility. No matter the path you choose to walk, there are costs. And we have to forgive each other—and ourselves—that's reality.

When Justin was six months old, there was a knock at the door. The woman introduced herself as a reporter from The Daily Mail. She asked if she could come in. I asked what it was she wanted. She said that she was writing a feature on mixed marriages. She asked, 'What did your parents think about you marrying an "Indian"?'

The tone and emphasis on 'Indian' was a slap to reality. It seemed possible that her aim was not to calm the fears of Daily Mail readers.

I replied, 'I didn't marry an Indian. I married Atam.' She looked none too pleased with my answer and left.

A neighbour showed me her copy of the feature. I was looking at a picture of our friend Graham, a good and kind man, in a turban. Graham had married Parvinder, a Sikh woman, and they'd had a Sikh wedding. In Enoch Powell's world if you were British, you could enjoy a British style wedding anywhere across the globe, but if you were in the UK and wanted a Sikh wedding then that was somehow a threat that fragmented society! The Daily Mail was mocking this pale-skinned, blond man wearing a turban. Fortunately Graham was comfortable in the Sikh community who embraced him, and his marriage was happy.

I was young but had wisely side-stepped that.

Justin loved being active. When he was little, I put him in a bouncing chair and kept him with me when I was working. We only had a twin-tub washing machine so laundry was time consuming but I'd talk to him or put on music. When he was three months we bought a baby bouncer and suspended it in the kitchen doorway. Perhaps that's why he was standing at seven months. Our next purchase, from a new company called Mothercare, was a baby walker. We only had a small backyard so most days I took him to Handsworth or Perry Vale parks, and let him dash about in the walker to the amusement of the old men chatting on the park benches. By nine months he was walking unaided.

Atam was awarded the MSc in Applied Maths to add to his MA in

Pure Maths. He was impressed by the new principal, Mr Brown, an ex-pilot of the Battle of Britain. He saw Atam's file and called him for a meeting. He said Atam deserved better and he would create a post of a Senior Lecturer in Maths for September 1969, which he should apply for and he doubted anyone more qualified would apply. The college had a branch in West Bromwich. The Bursar invited Atam for lunch and told him that he, not Mr Brown, would be in charge of that branch and he would have to work with him. The chair of the governors was a Welshman. He'd asked a relation from Wales to apply for the post. At that interview the chairman spoke to him in Welsh and afterwards insisted on appointing him, even though he only had an undergraduate degree and less experience than Atam. A year later we read that the Wednesbury bursar had been arrested for stealing college money.

Atam felt he had no option but to apply for other jobs and was appointed to the post of Senior Lecturer at the about-to-be-created Oxford Polytechnic, later called Oxford Brookes University. I was ecstatic about the idea of moving to Oxford. Atam was an exceptionally good teacher. When Atam took early retirement from Oxford Brookes, some of his students said to me that there had been five outstanding teachers at Brookes and Atam was one of them.

News came from India that left Atam in tears; the first time I'd seen him sob. His brother, Roshan, had died unexpectedly. Roshan had been the project manager, working free for the developer of an estate called Mansrover Gardens in Delhi in exchange for a plot of land on which to build a family home. He had borrowed to start a small factory manu-facturing transistor radios. Roshan and Urmila had four children. She needed money immediately to finish the house and pay off the debts. We sent what savings we had and the favourable exchange rate meant that their immediate problems were solved. But we had little to spare when we set up in our new home in Kennington, outside Oxford.

Vegetarian Moussaka 4-6 people

Justin likes to cook this for us

If you are in a supermarket and you see a trolley with a couple of aubergines, cans of borlotti beans and red wine, Justin is probably nearby. This is Justin's favourite.

Main sauce

Either olive oil or butter
A large onion – finely chopped
3 or 4 cloves of crushed garlic
2 cans of chopped tomatoes
Optional: one large glass of red wine (Spanish is Justin's favourite for this dish but Italian or Argentinian malbec are also very good)
Lots of dry mixed herbs: 3 tablespoons oregano, 1 and a half tablespoons of basil, half a tablespoon thyme
2 cans of borlotti beans (can add one tin of another bean type e.g. black beans are good)

To make the sauce, fry the finely chopped onion and crushed garlic until golden brown in the olive oil or butter. If you would like to make the dish a little more sophisticated, add finely chopped mushrooms and cook for a further 3 minutes. Add the cans of chopped tomatoes, wine and mixed herbs and cook on a medium heat for 10 minutes so that a good amount of the liquid evaporates. While the sauce is still relatively liquid, add the beans and cook for 5 minutes. Use a potato masher to mash about a third of the beans and cook for a few more minutes.

Aubergines

A large finely sliced aubergine

Cook both sides of all the sliced aubergines in either a griddle pan or under a grill. Be very careful if you use a grill as it is very easy to burn the aubergines. When slightly char-grilled the aubergines are done – set aside to cool. It takes about 15 minutes to grill the lot and I usually multi-task while making the main sauce above.

Top sauce

500 grams of natural yoghurt

300 grams of grated cheddar cheese

1 free range egg

Start with around a quarter of both the yoghurt and cheese and mix using a fork. Slowly add more continuing to mix with a fork. Once halfway break the egg and the yoke and egg-white into the mix. Keep mixing until all the yoghurt and cheese has been added.

Final stage

Place the main sauce in a large dish and then layer the aubergines on top. Pour the top source to cover the aubergines and place the large dish into a preheated oven and cook at 190 degrees for around 30-40 minutes. It is ready when a good proportion of the top is brown. Enjoy with a salad.

CHAPTER 12: Kennington 1970

Kennington is two miles from the beautiful city of Oxford and four miles from Abingdon, which claims to be the oldest town in Britain in continuous settlement. The village is squeezed into a narrow track of land between Bagley Woods and the River Thames. The ancient woodland was first mentioned in an Abbey Charter of 955CE by which King Eadred granted certain lands including Bagley Wood to the Abbot of Abingdon Abbey. It must have been a lawless place in the 13th century when men were frequently assaulted and sometimes killed in Bagley Wood and, in 1327 the prior of the abbey was carried off into the wood and threatened with a horrible end unless he did the prior-napper's bidding.

It didn't feel threatening to me, more like a huge weight had lifted and knots of tension eased. An optimistic current flowed like the Thames, which was visible from the back-bedroom window of our detached, fifties home. There were mostly private bungalows at the top end, council housing in the middle and where we lived, a mixture of private and council. Six months later at a coffee morning in a house opposite the church, I was asked by the host where I lived. I replied that we had moved next door to John and Eileen Keep, whom I expected she knew as John and his father had built rows of houses in the village.

'Oh,' she said, 'I don't know anyone on that side of the road!'

So the village was not without snobbery. Class in England is never far from the surface. Eileen Keep became like a mother to me. I felt lucky.

We had a long garden and the previous owner had preferred it productive. There was a tiny square lawn at the top followed by a forty feet long vegetable plot and an orchard. I set about redesigning it. Fortunately the soil was not heavy and I was able to do the work myself. I dug wavy borders and extended the lawn – almost a figure of eight and planted ornamental trees, shrubs and perennial plants, a sand pit for Justin and kept a small vegetable plot near the orchard. Atam got advice from Mr Keep on how to build a patio and we enjoyed the satisfaction of completing a building project.

We knocked down the dividing wall between the lounge and the dining room to make a spacious room. The house didn't have central heating and we didn't have the funds to install it, but there were two gas fireplaces and it wasn't cold. We added a heater in the hall which spread warmth upstairs. I painted it all in magnolia, as was the fashion. Atam's life was focussed on setting up the degree course in Maths, Stats and Computing.

A year later, Atam scared me: he passed out. The stress of having to create two courses from scratch was probably the cause. Our empathetic GP, Dr Blackman, prescribed a week off with lots of sleep and some exercise and he soon recovered, and it never happened again. We joined the Kennington Badminton Club and Atam played squash at the Polytechnic, which helped keep him fit. He bought a moped as the cheapest and easiest way of travelling the three and a half miles to the Polytechnic.

We couldn't afford to pay a babysitter but discovered the village babysitting groups, one at the Abingdon end and the other at the Oxford end. Our group had fourteen members which meant that, every fourteenth month I was responsible for the bookkeeping. It was like a bank statement of the assets and overdrafts of each member and, with the responsibility to organise the sits, you began by asking the debtors. The group met for a coffee morning once a month so we got to know each other and the children. I was told about the Women's Register with organised talks and events, where we weren't allowed to chat about our offspring. That was where I first heard about Women's Lib and where I met my first village friend.

Betsy Bell was an artist and her husband, David, a geologist and they had a son, Sam, who was the same age as Justin. Kennington was the village of choice for Oxford University's geology department, including Keith Cox, Steven Moorbath and John Dewey, who was one of the geologists behind plate tectonics. When the Bells had a sabbatical, they let their house to Stephen Jay Gould and his first wife, Deborah. There are few scientists famous enough in their life time to be canonised by the US Congress as a 'Living Legend' but that happened to Steve. In 1997, he even voiced a cartoon version of himself on *The Simpsons*.

Steve and Deborah joined the babysitting group, and Atam and I invited them to dinner and they returned the compliment. Atam and Steve discovered they had common interests in evolution and in wanting to expose scientific racism. Atam was hoping to get the opportunity to work on his longed-for PhD. The delay was auspicious because Atam's interest had turned towards quantitative genetics, and that would be his means of exposing the frauds.

In the 1960s, Steve was active in the civil rights movement. In 1963, he had attended Leeds University as a visiting undergraduate and organised weekly demonstrations outside a Bradford dance hall, which refused to admit black people. Unsurprisingly, the Goulds were against the Vietnam War, which was still raging, the US-backed overthrow of the democratic government of Chile and installation of General Pinochet, and what appeared to be the Belgium and US alliance to overthrow another democrat, Patrice Lumumba, the first prime minister of Democratic Republic of Congo. It was a dark time.

I asked them, 'Given American foreign policy, wouldn't you prefer to stay in the UK?'

Steve gave such an effective put down of the UK in relation to the world that I remember it to this day. 'Why would you want to ride the tiddler if you can ride the whale?'

For someone of my generation, this was a staggering perspective. It left me literally breathless. Britain: a tiddler.

We had been in the village about two months when there was a knock on the door. It was the vicar, Rev Harold Bennett, so I asked him in. He held out his hand to shake and said, 'I saw your husband.' Atam was the first brown-skinned person to live in the village so was noticeable. Harold meant no offence: it was his way of welcoming us. Apologising, I explained that Atam was a Hindu and I was an agnostic. 'Although I appreciate you calling, it's unlikely that you will see us in church.'

He wasn't put off by my bluntness but replied, 'As the parish priest everyone is my parishioner regardless of their faith or none.' I liked him. With two good GPs, friendly churches, two pubs, a village hall and lots of societies, Kennington felt like a strong community. It felt like home. And it has been my home ever since.

Once we'd settled in, I looked for work but there was a lack of nurseries and child care was hard to find. To work, a woman had to already be wealthy enough to afford a nanny. So I applied for a local authority post running a playgroup five mornings a week. I explained that Justin would have to come with me. I was delighted when they agreed.

I received exciting news. The world was becoming more connected. Joy oh joy, the brother I thought I'd never see again was coming home. Going to Australia or Australians coming here is no big deal in the twenty-first century but in 1970, only the rich could do it. Newly arrived Mike took eighteen-month-old Justin onto the cinder track at East Oxford and they both ran a lap savouring the memory of 6 May 1954 when Roger Bannister succeeded in breaking the four-minute mile with the help of his friends—the two Chrises. Mike and I had watched it on the seven-inch TV. While we knew it was possible, there was nothing inevitable about the race. It was truly inspirational and had signalled the idea that all things were possible, although the possibility that I would meet Roger Bannister was absurd. When Sir Roger graced the launch of my book, *Oxford Castaways*, in 2012 and made the closing speech, I told that story and introduced Mike to his hero: an unforgettable tear-jerker of a moment.

Mike and I meeting after ten years apart.

The main food story in this chapter is a sausage. In the newspaper photograph, Justin was holding one, except it's on a stick. Seventies sophistication was things on cocktail sticks: cheese, pineapple, cheese and pineapple on the same stick. At the age of eight, Justin decided to stop eating animals but continued for a year to eat mini sausages on a stick, not realising they were meat.

Atam and I wanted a brother or sister for Justin, so were pleased when, as before, we conceived quickly. But it wasn't to be and I miscarried. Nothing can quite prepare you for seeing a ten-week-old embryo outside your womb and the feeling of hollowness within. No words came to me, only shock and sadness that I didn't want Justin to see. I was helped through the grief by one of my oldest and kindest friends, Simonetta Agnello Hornby.

The odds on Atam and I meeting were almost zero, similar with the odds of me meeting Simonetta. What were the chances of a Sicilian from the wealthy landed gentry and a working-class girl from Luton meeting and becoming dear friends? I discovered her status as it was not something she cared about. Neither could Simonetta envisage that one day she would become one of Italy's most celebrated authors.

Simonetta's oldest son, George, was born a year before we met. She and her husband Martin, had met in Cambridge, married, moved to the USA to study (Martin at Harvard Business School) and then to Zambia, where Martin advised the newly independent government on how to build its economy. And then back to the UK. In 2021, it is hard to conceive of a nationalised British car firm but that was the case with the partly Oxford-based British Leyland. And it wasn't thriving in comparison with its German and US rivals. Martin had the job of analysing the situation.

What were the chances of us buying houses in the same street which meant we were likely to encounter each other? The name Vetta is rare in India but well known in Italy and Atam looked rather Sicilian so perhaps it was meant to be. That is a bit of Indian fatalism, although Atam was no longer Indian: he'd become a naturalised Brit just before Justin's birth.

On my first visit to her bungalow, I was let in by an au pair and the indelible vision was of Simonetta with the Law of Tort on her lap, George playing quietly on the floor between her legs and her pipe on the table beside her—completely unforgettable. My admiration for her began in that moment. Simonetta had an Italian law degree from Palermo University and was studying to become a British solicitor. To do that with George and pregnant with her next son, Nicolas, was impressive.

After the au pair left, her pregnancy hit a danger and she was advised to stay in bed. A neighbour across the road, who sometimes worked as a child carer, looked after George. Take-away food is ubiquitous today but not in 1971, so I delivered meals to her. After my miscarriage she returned the favour.

There is a reminder of Simonetta every time I walk into my dining room: my set of Art Nouveau dining chairs. When Atam and I set up home we had £50 to buy everything from the pots and pans to the furniture, carpets and curtains, and that wasn't much even in those days. White melamine was the fashion in the sixties but we'd searched Birmingham's second-hand shops and bought six C19th captain's chairs for ten shillings each (50p). By the early seventies, the tide of dislike for Victorian and Edwardian furniture was turning, so Simonetta and I were ahead of the curve. Those chairs were far too big for our Kennington house, so I sold them for the princely sum of £4 each to an Oxford dealer.

We enjoyed shopping for fresh food together on market day in Oxpens, and exploring antiques and second-hand shops. She spotted the sad-looking Art Nouveau chairs with springs hanging out and dirty torn upholstery in a warehouse on the outskirts of Witney. They cost me £4 each and an extra £4 each to be re-upholstered in turquoise, but I loved them then and love them today.

When I became pregnant with Adrian, our second son, the world of obstetrics was changing. The days of 'Call the Midwife' when the midwife traditionally shared an intimate, emotional experience, were threatened. Male obstetricians thought progress meant mechanising the processes of birth, preferably inducing between 9.00 am and 5.00 pm. That was going to have a profound impact on me.

Finishing touches were being put to the new John Radcliffe Maternity Hospital so my first prenatal examination was in the Old Radcliffe Infirmary. It was embarrassing. When I was called to the desk the sister went through my particulars in a voice loud enough for everyone in the waiting room to hear said, 'This is your third pregnancy. One birth and one abortion.'

I objected saying, 'It was a miscarriage.'

She replied, 'It's the same thing.' Now that's a bedside manner.

Modern techniques were revolutionising obstetrics. At six months I was given a scan and a urine test in the shining bright hospital on a hill and both results, I was informed, were excellent. I'd only experienced minor morning sickness, the sun was shining and life was good.

At seven months that all changed. After his examination of me, the registrar informed me that he wanted me to come in at 37 weeks for an early induction.

'Why?' I asked.

'Because your first baby was small.'

Justin had been only five and a half pounds.

I replied, 'Doesn't it make sense to keep this baby in the womb longer to grow more?'

'A baby can be alive in the womb at 36 weeks and dead at 39 weeks,' he said. It is hard to describe my distress. I'd tried to be strong but was exposed as utterly vulnerable. I made an appointment to see my GP and asked Dr Blackman if he could help me. Could I give birth in the new GP unit on the top floor of the new maternity hospital, where he and a community midwife could deliver my baby at full term?'

Because his was a single-man practice, it was not an option for him. What was I to do? I wanted to scream 'NO! NO! NO! I want this baby to be born naturally in his/her own good time.' At the next consultation, the registrar was even more insistent. How could I go against medical advice? What if something did go wrong?

We hit on a compromise. I agreed to come into hospital early but he wouldn't induce the baby unless necessary. He suggested a new procedure, an amniocentesis to confirm everything was healthy. It seemed like the only option. Mum and Dad came to look after Justin. After three days they did the amniocentesis. My emotions were at full pelt. In the hours on end in a hospital bed, I wrote oodles of poetic drivel about Mother Nature being subverted and of female helplessness in the face of male authority.

A trainee female obstetrician was sent to talk me into having an induction. I explained my stance. 'There's a reason why pregnancy is forty weeks. That is the way nature intended it.'

I sensed that she sympathised with my point of view but couldn't contradict the registrar. Two days later, I was saved by the big chief returning from the USA. Professor Stallworthy, the registrar, his assistant and three students gathered around my bed. When Professor Stallworthy asked me how I felt, I felt naked, but I struggled to be convincing and repeated my contention that the pregnancy was healthy and I should be allowed to continue to full term.

He tapped lightly on my arm and said, 'You're a fit young woman, your baby is healthy and I don't see why you shouldn't go home and come back when it's ready.'

The registrar's face was a sight to behold, looking more than annoyed, but I could have kissed the professor. The good thing was that, when I went into labour, the registrar stayed away. I was put in the charge of a delightful midwife. She asked if a student could be there and I agreed. Afterwards she explained that mine was the first natural delivery that she had witnessed.

The birth was easy compared with Justin and the midwife was kind and caring, unlike the aggressive Birmingham lady. Atam saw the moment when Adrian emerged into the world announcing his presence with a call of the wild. The relief after the stress of the previous two months and the simple joy of being able to hold him right away and have him with me on the ward felt like a gift from a god I didn't believe in.

In the seventies, women were not meant to be in charge of our bodies. Unknown to me, I was one of the many, *many* women who wanted things to change. I later met the campaigner for natural childbirth, Sheila Kitzinger, who famously said, 'For far too many, pregnancy and birth is still something that happens to them rather than something they set out consciously and joyfully to do themselves.'

When my third son, Paul, was born in 1974, there must have been notes on my record because no one suggested early induction and it was another natural delivery with only midwives present. Between Justin and Paul there'd been a good development. When I had breast-fed Justin, I was the only mother on the ward not bottle feeding so the nurse drew a curtain around me. With Paul, in a bay of six new mothers, two others were breastfeeding with no curtains to keep us out of sight.

More positive changes were to come, although I didn't know it at the time. Obstetrics was becoming more mother-friendly, breastfeeding better supported and children of mixed race less rare. By 2070, more than half the population of the UK will be of mixed ancestry. They will insist on being judged as individuals and not be defined by a particular label.

This chapter has mostly been a delight to write laced with love, friendship and optimism. Prejudice in a place like Oxford was unspoken. Simonetta passed on some comments of a few members of the Women's Register, who had told her that they couldn't understand why I had married an 'Indian'. I don't doubt that my life would have been even harder had I wed an African. Discrimination on the basis of colour became illegal in the UK but that law hadn't wiped out centuries of programming. In 1735, the Swedish botanist Carl Linnaeus revolutionised the way plants, animals and other objects from the natural world were named and classified. The original C18th collection of the British Museum shows how advancing Western science wanted to categorise hierarchically everything, including religion. Empire and enlightenment grew together and the result was that people too were categorised. In the seventies, from the grass roots to the highest reaches of society, it was still the norm.

At 3.00 am one morning, there was a deafening banging on our door. We worried that it would wake up Adrian and Justin, so both of us hurried to open it. Two large, burly police officers were stood there.

'What can we do for you, officers?' asked Atam.

'We are looking for Justin Vetta,' was the astounding reply.

'My son is asleep upstairs. Why are you looking for him?' I asked.

'We have a report that he was involved in football hooliganism.'

'Do you know how old our son is?'

Of course they knew. But I smiled at them as they left, knowing that they had wanted to intimidate us and I didn't want them to think they had succeeded. They no doubt wanted Atam to go 'back home' so they would've been pleased that in three months' time we headed for India.

Adrian is the only one of my sons not to become vegetarian but in recent years he has eaten little meat. Here's his healthy breakfast.

Adrian's Muesli

7 cups rolled oats (or mix of grains: wheat bran, rye, barley)

1 cup pumpkin Seeds

1 cup sunflower Seeds

1 cup currants

1 cup unsweetened Coconut Flakes

1 cup almond flakes

1/2 cup chia seed

1/2 cup hemp hearts

Optional: whatever you like.

I like berries and yoghurt

CHAPTER 13: A Taste of India 1973

It took three years to save enough for the fares to India. It cost as much in 1973 as it does today, but given lower salaries back then, it was expensive! At only seven months old, Adrian went free. As well as the usual vaccines, we had to have inoculations against small pox, as it was still a scourge. We let our house for three months to a friendly visiting Australian academic and his family to cover our expenses.

Although Kuwait Airlines refuelled in the Gulf and we were allowed off the plane, I was pretty exhausted when we landed in Delhi. A long flight without in-flight entertainment was not easy with young children. I wasn't looking my best as we headed for customs and immigration. Indian bureaucracy works at a slow pace. You couldn't exchange sterling for rupees in the UK, so getting through customs, changing money and collecting our luggage took a long time.

I wasn't expecting the reception that greeted us. Beneath sun-drenched skies, twenty members of the family were waiting eager to greet Atam and meet his new family. It felt as if we were royalty, except that I certainly didn't look like it! We were to stay for the first few days with a better-off cousin who had built a three-storey house. The traditional multi-generational house was around a courtyard but that didn't work in cities so each generation occupied one level. One was given up to accommodate us.

No brownie points for knowing the location of this pic.

We did the usual sight-seeing in Delhi: the Red Fort, which had been the heart of the Mughal Empire, and Lutyens New Delhi, the final head-quarters of the Raj. There are almost as many Indias as there are Indians.

Even today, there are remote 'tribal' communities and people with a Stone-Age culture in the Andamans as well as a space programme and cutting-edge institutions similar to MIT in Boston, where my seven-month-old baby would later study for his PhD. Even in 1973, we enjoyed a means of transport not then available in the UK. We travelled to Agra on the Taj Express, an electrified train with airline style seating.

A family birthday party a few days after we arrived remains a strong memory. Birthday parties were not a traditional Hindu celebration but they were becoming fashionable with the middle classes. There was a western birthday cake with candles sitting in the middle of the table surrounded by aromatic samosas, *chaats* and *pakoras* and laughter-inducing pani-puree, but in pride of place in front of them all was a bottle of Heinz tomato ketchup. It was on display as a symbol of affluence and sophistication because it was exotic and expensive in 1973 India.

The young woman whose birthday it was asked if she could see my clothes and jewellery. She was to be disappointed: apart from my engagement and wedding rings I had no jewellery. Later in life, I developed a liking for Scandinavian silver jewellery and colourful costume pieces but at that time, I had zilch. She was equally disenchanted by my clothes. I'd bought with me three long skirts. In the sixties, my outfits of choice were mini-skirts. I knew minis in India would reinforce prejudices so I bought Laura Ashley maxi skirts in trendy autumn colours.

Her disillusionment was unmistakeable. I explained that I hoped to buy a couple of saris while I was in Delhi and asked if she would help me to choose and show me how to wear them. We went to Ramesh Nagar and bought a cream cotton sari and a blue silk sari, but the tailor also made me a pair of *lungi*, full trousers that looked like a skirt. I loved the glamourous emerald-green raw silk. Silk can feel cool or warm, and yet it is as light as gossamer.

I was not surprised that the Delhi ladies were unimpressed with my skirts. The autumn colours looked drab in the Indian sunlight. In the British Midlands, the bright saris of some Indian ladies looked garish, whereas in India they look stunning. It's all about the light. It reminded me of my father and our love of Cornwall and why artists settle there: the light.

I learned more about my husband's past. When Atam had become a lecturer in a private school funded by a wealthy industrialist, he and his wife visited and suggested that Atam become engaged to their daughter. The wedding was arranged for the summer holidays. Nearing the time, they asked to postpone because their son had been taken seriously ill with kidney failure. Atam hadn't met his heiress fiancée and assumed they were having second thoughts because he wasn't rich. That coincided with him seeing the advert for the post in Ethiopia and he never returned to India. When he told me this story, I thought he was crazy.

He could've been married to the part-owner of a steel mill and a hotel, and instead chose a girl from Luton without a penny to her name. When I wrote *Sculpting the Elephant* I wanted this reversal of Western expectations. My English hero, Harry, had to struggle for everything he owned, whereas the Indian heroine, Ramma, didn't have to worry about money.

Krishan was honest with me that the family had been disappointed because the marriage would have been a good connection for the extended family. He also asked what my parents thought of us marrying. A general discussion about mixed marriages followed and I understood why South Asians had problems in Africa. Indian attitudes to black people were not so different to that of the prejudiced white in the seventies. While Atam's family didn't believe in caste or in dowries, that was not the prevailing opinion. Most Indians did not approve of marrying outside caste.

∞

That trip was the only one to India in which I was taken ill. Safe bottled water was not available in 1973. I tried to stick to filtered water and bottled fizzy drinks, although I don't like them, but my downfall was when the family offered me ice. On subsequent trips I avoided ice and washed salad, and I even brushed my teeth in bottled water. Cured but drained of energy, it affected me breastfeeding Adrian. I had to up his intake of solid food and use milk in a cup. Trying to ensure the milk and containers were sterile while travelling made me anxious, which was why I'd tried to keep up the breastfeeding.

All travellers at that time will have loo stories to tell. In Delhi, the homes we stayed in had flush toilets but in Ludhiana it was a hole in the floor above an open sewer. A shower was a jug dipped in a bucket of water which you threw over yourself and the water went down the hole. That was bad enough but improvements were being made and main drainage was being installed. The pneumatic drills digging up the street dispersed dirt and disease into the air. That was how I contracted bacterial pneumonia.

Before that I had another dose of Delhi belly. Kundan prescribed something that made me well but when he took my pulse, he looked at me strangely. I asked what was the matter and he replied, 'I think you are pregnant.'

Ade was only eight months old and I was still breast feeding. So I doubted it. Kundan arranged for me to be examined by a woman doctor. It was to be an unpleasant experience. She and her attendants thought I knew no Hindi. Racism is not just a white disease.

When I was expecting Justin, I hoped we could bring him up bilingual. I asked Atam to teach me but as he was at university in the morning and teaching in the afternoon and evening he had no time. I scoured the bookshops and eventually found *Teach Yourself Hindustani*. I learnt the Hindi alphabet and practiced the sounds. Then I started learning the phrases. One weekend I asked Atam to help me practice. He was horrified.

'You can't talk to my family like that!'

He examined the book and discovered the problem. It was published in the early forties for the ruling English Sahibs and Memsahibs to give orders to their servants. Hindi is a respectful language. For example, you don't say 'Daddy' you say 'Daddy-ji', that is, 'respected father'. There was precious little respect in this book. I abandoned it, but in India I listened hard and, in that surgery, it was easy to tell kindness and respect from insults and sneering, both in words and gestures.

I was struggling to come to terms with being pregnant when I became seriously ill. A doctor educated in Western medicine diagnosed the pneumonia, and told Atam that I could die. It was through that doctor that I discovered why I had problems being understood. That generation of Indians had learned English from thirties text books so they said 'I am not, you cannot, they are not'– not 'I'm' or 'can't' or 'aren't'. I was shocked to realise that almost every other sentence I spoke involved a contraction. Atam had naturally reverted to Indian English (Hinglish) as well as speaking Hindi while we were there, so they understood him but knew he was an expat! Once the penicillin began to take effect, we booked flights home, one month early, the planned holiday in Kashmir abandoned.

Atam and I had very much wanted one more child but hadn't anticipated it quite so soon. Once back home in Kennington, I made an appointment to see Dr Blackman and was relieved that our baby was growing normally and it was unlikely that the pneumonia and penicillin would have affected him because they happened after the three-month mark. It took a while to regain my strength and I'd need it. There was to be only fourteen months between Adrian and Paul.

Recipe Alloo Tikki Chaat (Serves 4:)

This is my daughter-in-law Amita's version which she demonstrated at the international zoom launch of the audiobook of Sculpting the Elephant. This is Indian cookery; it's jazz not Classical Music so you can improvise!

Ingredients:

8 large potatoes, one small onion, two fresh green chillis (or half teaspoon red chilli powder), one teaspoon garam masala, half teaspoon salt, handful freshly chopped coriander (or half teaspoon coriander powder), one teaspoon mango powder (amchoor).

Method:

Chop and boil the potatoes in salted water. Once boiled until soft, drain and put in a mixing bowl, adding all the ingredients. Once cooled down, form patty shapes from the spicy mashed potato, then coat in all-purpose flour.

Heat some oil in a frying pain and shallow fry the potato patties until golden brown. For best results, make the patties from mash made the day before.

For the Chaana (Chick Pea Curry)

This keeps really well and tastes better on the second day! If you haven't got every ingredient adapt...

Two tins boiled chick peas

Half tin tomatoes

One large onion, one tablespoon ginger garlic paste, or one inch ginger & two cloves garlic. All chopped.

Two tablespoons oil for frying

One teaspoon cumin seeds, one teaspoon garam masala , half teaspoon turmeric powder , half teaspoon chilli powder, half teaspoon salt , one teaspoon mango powder (amchoor)

Fresh coriander added at the end

Method

Fry the cumin seeds in the oil, until golden brown.

Add the chopped onion, ginger garlic and fry until soft and brown.

Add the tomatoes, along with all the spices, frying until you see that the oil has separated from the spicy tomato and onion mixture.

Add the chick peas, stir until all the chick peas are coated in the tomato mixture.

Add maybe half a cup of water, stir, and bring to the boil. Once brought to the boil, stir, cover and simmer for around 45 mins or until the chick pea mixture has softened.

CHAPTER 14: Deeply Local and Sicily

My parents came to help but when my labour began, they went down with an awful bout of flu. I looked after them because my labour was progressing slowly. At 2.00 am the following morning, I had no choice but to head for the hospital, alone; Atam couldn't come with me because of Justin and Adrian. Our lovely neighbour, Eileen Keep, took them in at 7.00 am so he just made the last seconds of labour. Paul was born with a smile and has kept it. I'm lucky. It felt like Jove was on my side when both Annie and Angie, my friends from teacher's college, set up home nearby.

When BBC Radio Oxford launched at the end of 1970, Angie's husband Thomas got work there. I first heard the Beatles on Radio Luxembourg, an increasingly popular pirate radio station. To stop them, the government asked the BBC to set up local stations. Bill Heine, whose shark house I mention in the Appetiser, was a presenter for more than thirty years. I not only cast him away on Oxtopia but was privileged to appear on his programmes many times, either as a guest presenter or to review the papers on a Sunday.

Thomas was one of the first Radio Oxford producers. His parents helped with a deposit so he and Angie were able to buy a house on the canal side of Kingston Road. Atam and I made a mental note, hoping that, when the time came, we could do the same for our children. Angie was pregnant with their first son when I was expecting Adrian (my second), but her experience was not like mine. Angie went on to be deeply involved in the National Childbirth Trust.

After Chris Wright was awarded his PhD in biochemistry, he and Annie lived for a while in Stockport. Our trip to visit them was the furthest north that I'd been. When Chris landed a post at the nearby government lab at Harwell, they bought a house in Abingdon. Annie was pregnant with her first child, Michael, when I was pregnant with Paul (my third). My focus at that time was local. In 1973, I was the founding chairwoman of the first mother-and-toddler group in Oxfordshire. It fulfilled a deep need and was instantly successful with parents travelling some distance, including Annie. It possibly laid the foundation to the close friendship that Paul and Michael enjoy today.

Paul and me at the toddler group I founded

∞

In 1976, Simonetta invited us to spend a month in Sicily at their family estate set in ancient olive groves—an unforgettable experience. It was early days of mass travel and we bought tickets on a chartered flight. Simonetta's sister, Chiara, later converted the stable block and turned the Mose estate into a business so you can see the house on their website.

This trip was an in-depth introduction to Italian cuisine. I learned how to cook pasta al dente, discovered basil, parmesan and home-made passata. The sights, smells and variety of the food markets of Palermo offered a palette of brilliant colours.

I wanted those wonderful ingredients to be available in England. A memorable food experience was of pizza in the land of its birth. In Mose, the village bakery had a stone oven where it came out piping hot with a sauce of tomatoes ripened in the Mediterranean sun, bubbling mozzarella and freshly picked basil—simple but perfect.

Simonetta's mother, Elena, was warm, welcoming and a delight to get to know. It was not easy for her that her daughter lived most of the time abroad. I never heard her complain; she adapted and was a constant loving presence in her grandsons' lives before computers, Skype and Zoom. Luckily for me, she was learning English.

Despite its sensuous beauty, rich cultural heritage and food like works of art, there was a dark side to this island at the crossroads of Europe, Africa and the Middle East. Simonetta used her understanding of Sicilian society in all its variety when she wrote her first novel, *La Mennulara* (The Almond Picker).

Recipes

I learned how to use left over pasta and a simple way of cooking aubergines

Fried Aubergines

Slice the aubergine and season the slices with garlic salt and black pepper. (Preferably leave them to stand for a little while.)

Dip the slices in wholemeal or plain flour so that both sides are covered.

Heat a frying pan and add a little olive oil and cook for five minutes over a moderate heat turning once. Optional: garnish with chopped flat leaf parsley.

Pasta Fritta

What to do with that leftover pasta?

Heat a little olive oil in a large frying pan or wok and add the leftover pasta.

Cook for a while turning it often using a spatula or wooden spoon.

Sprinkle on a mixture of grated mozzarella and parmesan and lower the heat.

Optional: stir in a couple of tablespoons of red pesto.

Serve once the cheese is browned and garnish with torn basil leaves.

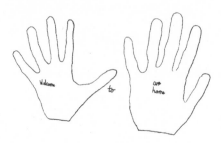

CHAPTER 15: Fopin Li & International Students

Meet the new member of the family: Fopin Li. After my brother, Mike, decided to return to the now more prosperous and optimistic UK, he soon found work at the Commonwealth Secretariat in London, and while there, he met an enterprising young woman from Mauritius.

Fopin's mother was born on the island but her father had arrived there from Shanghai in the late thirties. He became the editor of the Chinese language newspaper in Port Louis. The language of Mauritius was French Creole and Fopin had been taught in a French Catholic school. In 1972, a few weeks before her twentieth birthday she left for Zambia to work as a secretary in the Ministry of Education, and from there she came to the UK in 1975.

We were first introduced to her in a shared house in Baron's Court. Even in those circumstances, Fo, as we started to call her, served up treats. We are familiar with the saying that *The French live to eat and the British eat to live.* That attitude has changed during my life time and thanks to Fopin, I became more familiar with the equally ardent Chinese food culture. She has a passion for cooking and is a superb chef. Mauritian food is to die for, prepared carefully, cooked quickly and enjoyed with a lingering aftertaste. The elegant Chinese presentation is enhanced with Indian spices.

Not long after meeting Fopin, we moved house. The tiny box room that had been Atam's study had become Paul's room and we could hardly get into our bedroom, which by then had to accommodate all of his books and files. There is a saying in Kennington that houses only come up for sale when someone dies and then a villager buys it. That's a generalisation but it was true for us.

Our opportunity came when a unique house came on the market after Mr Walker, the man who had built it, died. If it hadn't been in a dreadful state we wouldn't have been in the running—a buyer with funds beyond our means would have snapped it up. Lots of people viewed it and loved the oak, the spacious rooms, large windows and good-sized garden but were put off by the amount of work that needed doing. Unusually for the time, it was timber framed. Mr Walker had bought land all the way to the railway line. One side of Kennington Road had two extensive workshops where he made the oak fittings used in Great Western Railway carriages. The house he'd built is held up by railway sleepers.

He left England for Canada at the outbreak of WWI and when he returned, met a local girl. But she wasn't keen to cross the pond. Mr Walker, as a wheelwright and joiner, built a bungalow and then kept on going until it was three stories high. There's plenty of evidence of his skills with wood and he knew how to build a Canadian-style, timber-framed and insulated house with eyebrows.

He'd bought the land at a significant time in the history of Kennington. The village is bounded by water meadows along a beautiful stretch of the Thames. One of the houses close to the local pub, known as the Manor House, was built in 1629, and most of the surrounding land was a tenanted estate. The Kennington Road was prone to flooding and so few new houses were built.

When Oxford accepted the Great Western Railway in 1844 and it crossed the farm, work was done to lessen the likelihood of an inundation. The modern history of the village began on May 13, 1913 when the estate was divided into 38 lots, which were put up for auction. The

Walkers bought one, on which he built our house. It was one of the first in the village to have a bathroom. The problem was that the cistern was wooden and leaked, and by the end of his life, everything was thoroughly flooded. He installed central heating with huge institutional radiators but the boiler was kaput. The dining room ceiling was hanging down and the roof sagged and worst of all for a timber framed house, it was riddled with woodworm. I won't go into detail about the kitchen.

Most people thought that, with such a young family, we were mad to take it on. If you don't grasp an opportunity when it's available, the chance is unlikely to come again. I went to see Mr Walker's daughter, Doreen, who was selling the house. I explained that seventy gallons of paraffin-based wood worm fluid needed to be sprayed on the timber framed house and all the plumbing and wiring needed replacing. The surveyor had said that we could use the sockets safely but he advised against using the lighting circuit. Before making our offer, I asked her to give us access on exchange of contracts. Work that could be dangerous for my youngest son, Paul, who was only four, could be done before we occupied the house.

Doreen lived in the village and I didn't think not to trust her. When the time came, she refused to give us the key and the promise wasn't in writing. We had to move in the day after the spraying. Our plumber sealed the loo so it was usable. A few days later a friend of Justin's came to see him. When he got home his mother phoned me. 'Have you spilled paraffin in the house because our Kevin's anorak is soaked with it? I asked his mother if it was raining. She agreed and I replied, 'I'm sorry, Mrs Cox, but all Kevin did was walk into our house and walk home in the rain.'

My brother Ray came up from Cornwall and did the rewiring with Atam as his gofer. We had a fabulous plumber, Gerald Cox, who fitted an immersion heater to get us by while he installed the central heating, renewed the gas piping and fitted a new bathroom.

Not having access after the exchange of contracts meant the kitchen was a challenge because we had to use it and work on it at the same time. It meant levelling half the floor then the other half before tiling it, plastering one wall at a time etc. Later I learned that I wasn't the only person to take Doreen at her word and live to regret it. The consequence: she goes down in a book as a deceiver.

Fopin and Mike had just moved in together in Wimbledon, and her parents came to the UK. They were among the first to visit our new home. Fo's parents didn't speak English but with lots of gesturing and smiles, we could communicate without language. Mum and Dad were staying and helping particularly with the garden. When Mike and Fo came with her parents, Uncle Charlie and Auntie Eva joined us. We sat on the floor in the dining room and enjoyed a feast which Fo's family had prepared in the dismally equipped kitchen. Uncle Charlie brought bottles of his homemade wine. It was a delightful day relived in this photo of Fo's parents and mine.

Kennington. My parents with Fopin's parents

We needed money to pay for materials and furniture so we decided to take in international language students and I gave one-to-one EFL lessons to those advanced students at a language school who needed specialist vocabulary. Young people coming to Oxford to learn English was a new phenomenon. Warnborough College had opened on Boars Hill and wanted host families. Our first guests were two glamorous Libyans, Samira and Iptesan. I decorated and bought attractive curtains for their double room. The dining room was looking respectable. The heavy oak draw leaf dining table I'd bought in Birmingham for £3 had come in useful. I stood on it, broom in hand, holding up a square of plaster board while Atam nailed it in place. We papered the ceiling so you couldn't see the join. Inventive, no?

Given our role in the overthrow of Colonel Gaddafi in 2011, it's strange to think that, in 1978, the British government encouraged the Libyan leader's programme of sending young people to experience Europe, funded by their new oil wealth. Iptesan introduced us to a red-hot chilli paste called harissa, which she spread thickly on toast. Samira was of Bedouin ancestry. Her family were prosperous. I looked surprised when she mentioned the family slave. People think of slavery as a thing of the past but it was and is alive and well. She couldn't comprehend my horror because she loved this woman.

She taught me how to prepare a traditional Bedouin dish called rishta. The nomads keep jars of dried lamb and make thin noodles to make the rishta. I make my own vegetarian version using pasta. It's like a veggie curry with different kinds of beans and pasta in a spicy tomato sauce. It became a favourite with the boys when they went to university. They could impress their friends by making a huge pan of it to cater for a party.

Our home may not have been a show house but the foreign students we had over the years enlivened our evening meals and our boys learned a lot from our lodgers. The world had come to us and soon the boys would go out into it. First, through a sabbatical in the USA.

Fopin's Mauritian Achard (Tumeric and Mustard preserved vegetables)

Ingredients

100g white cabbage
100g carrots
100g green beans
1 small onion, white or red either is fine
3 cloves of garlic
About 1/2 to 1 cup of olive oil or more if needed
2 tbsp mustard seeds
green chillies (slice them lengthwise) - amount of chillies depend on your 'best' preference.
2 tsp ground turmeric
salt to taste

Method

Slice thinly (lengthwise) the cabbage, carrots and green beans.

Add about 3 tablespoons of salt to the veggies, mix it, and let it sit for about 15 minutes to 1hr.

While the veggies are soaking in salt finely chop the onions and crush the garlic cloves.

Add about 1/2 a cup of olive oil in a big mixing bowl.

Add the garlic, turmeric, green chillies, onions and the crushed garlic. Season with a little bit of salt.

After an hour or so, the veggies would have released some water due to the sodium. It's normal. Next step is to squeeze as much of the water out using a cloth or just between your hands.

After you squeeze most of the liquid off the veggies, add them to the spice and oil mix.

Mix all the ingredients well.

Store in an airtight container adding some more oil on top to prevent mould.

The 'achard' is now ready to be eaten but it is best to serve it the following day to allow the flavours to mature. You can leave it on the countertop for 2-3 days then it can be stored in the fridge for about 2 weeks. Or put it in the fridge straight away.

This 'achard' can be served as a side dish, with rice or on sandwiches, baguettes, whatever you prefer. It is a very popular dish in Mauritius. We call it 'di pain zazar' in creole, which is the Mauritian patois we speak. 'Di pain zazar' means 'bread with achard'.

WOMEN'S LIB
G
K   B
ANTI-APARTHEID
I   D
D   S
S

CHAPTER 16: Misogyny, CND and KADS

A major culture clash rippled through the next decade: the divergence was over sex and gender. The split crossed colour, class and cultures. I watched with sadness as families, communities and institutions fractured. It was also an education for me.

The majority in the South Asian and the religious Afro/Caribbean communities sided with a certain Mary Whitehouse, who claimed to represent Christian and family values. Appalled and worried about women's new roles and changing sexual mores, she advocated strict censorship and criminalising (or the blocking of decriminalising) certain sex acts. There were many who equally passionately felt that those traditional values had been used to oppress women and the LGBT community. Consensual homosexual acts were only decriminalised in 1967. In the eighties, 'coming out' was not only difficult, leading to break-ups with families and damage to careers, but it could be dangerous. People were dying of AIDS, which the Daily Mail branded as 'The Gay Plague'. The fear and prejudice are now hard to imagine. Sufferers were treated like lepers. That is why the photograph of Princess Diana holding the hand of an AIDS patient made such an impact.

I never expected to meet people from the heart of it, to hear their stories first hand, but in 2013, I interviewed the film producer, Victor

Glynn, who described to me a controversy in 1982 which made headlines in the national press. Charges of gross indecency were brought by Mary Whitehouse against Victor's friend, Michael Bogdanov, who was then the associate director of The National Theatre. His most recent play, 'Romans in Britain', featured a male rape scene and Mr Bogdanov faced up to two years in prison if convicted.

The prosecution argument rested partly on whether an act that *appears* to be a crime on stage should be treated as if it *were* a crime. They knew they were in trouble when tested on the legalities of *Macbeth* and hilariously, Agatha Christie's *The Mousetrap*. Their case was further troubled by the fact that Mrs Whitehouse had never actually seen the production.

In 1982, while the trial at the Old Bailey was in progress, Victor reproduced the proceedings every night at The Oxford Playhouse.

We employed the fastest shorthand writer we could find, Ruth Kibble, and she took it all down for us. On the train back to Oxford, she transcribed it with Guy Hibbert, the Playhouse's writer in residence, who then edited it. It was then read live on stage at 10.30. Hosted by yours truly each night, the production was covered on Newsnight on BBC2 by its very glamorous arts correspondent, Joan Bakewell. Assuming the role of the judge was the Star Wars' Lord Palpatine himself, Ian McDiarmid.

On day two, Mary Whitehouse's solicitor issued proceedings against Victor for contempt of court. The trial ended with the intervention of the Attorney General.

The whole imbroglio was farcical. And oh-so-English. We argue things out on stage. There's a joke that if three Englishmen were washed up on a desert isle, two would create a theatre company and one would be the audience.

And, sure enough, I've fulfilled my national stereotype. In 2014, Victor, my friend Polly Biswas Gladwin, an award-winning feminist filmmaker and I organised the Shakespeare in Oxford Project. We brought together twenty young people from diverse backgrounds to workshop 'Joe and Sara', Polly's contemporary take on 'Romeo and Juliet'. Those teenagers were impressive. The more I get to know their generation, despite myself, I am infected by hope. They would feel totally alienated by the prejudices I've regularly encountered.

In 1971 I helped to found Kennington Amateur Dramatic Society (KADS) with me as chair and Shirley Jones—a talented writer—as vice chair. After two successful years, I explained to the Annual General Meeting that Atam had a sabbatical coming up in the States so this would be my last year as chairman. A male parish councillor stood up and said, 'That's good. We don't like women telling us what to do.'

This was one of many put downs I've experienced throughout my life. Nowadays, it's called a micro-aggression. They were incessant, but not as bad as the sexist 'banter' that many women in male-dominated professions have had to endure. But it's a good example of the dilemma that faces women. His was an off-the-cuff comment, a throw-away line by a local leader that was meant to be funny. And indeed, several people duly chuckled. If I'd said something cutting back, then I'd have been the one creating a scene and lacking a sense of humour.

I said nothing, just like every other time before and many times since. Looking back over my life, I've asked myself if, by being silent about that crap, I made myself complicit.

∞

About the same time, Atam wanted to bring together Oxford residents of South Asian ancestry from different religious persuasions. The aim was to involve both men and women. The first gathering was in our front room. It felt somewhat awkward because the Muslim women said not a word. The idea was to go around to each other's homes. Ours was intended as the ice breaker. The second gathering at the home of a Hindu shopkeeper seemed to bear out our optimism, but the third came as a shock. We were to be entertained by a Muslim family in East Oxford. The moment the door was opened, Atam was ushered into the front room with the men and I was directed to the rear of the house with the women.

As we drove home, I apologised to Atam. 'I'm sorry but I can't be part of this.'

It's hard to adjust one's perspective and overcome barriers to change. Change takes time, patience and compassion. Someone who has that is the Rev Charlotte Bannister Parker (Sir Roger Bannister's daughter). Charlotte started the Faith Walk which takes place every June. It begins at the synagogue where it is usually a woman who leads the prayer. We march to St Giles Church and listen to the choir and then move on to St Mary the Virgin where the Indian religions chant. That section is often organised by family friend, Chinta Kalli. The walk ends with prayer and supper at the mosque. Charlotte has created channels of communication that reveal how much we have in common as well as our differences.

The year after Atam's group collapsed, he was approached by the minister of the Church of South India to help ease a difficult situation. The son of the minister and a Muslim girl had fallen in love. She knew her parents would prevent the match, so they had eloped to Gretna Green. Some in the local Muslim community were furious and set alight the church's mini-bus and the minister received threats on his life. The bush telegraph went full blast and the couple were found, abducted and brought back to Oxford. She was sent to Pakistan for a forced marriage. With such bigoted passions, there was nothing Atam could do.

While most cultural practices are a delight to share, some abominations such as forced marriage, female oppression and female genital mutilation have been tolerated for far too long in the name of multiculturalism. Liberalism must have its boundaries, and there must be universal human rights.

When we returned from our sabbatical in 1982, Shirley and I put our heads together to come up with an exciting theatre programme for young people. In 1979, the decision was made to deploy US Cruise and Pershing missiles in Britain and several other Western European countries. Their deployment at nearby Upper Heyford and Greenham Common was causing lots of protests. I joined CND (the Campaign for Nuclear Disarmament), and Shirley and I were among the 30,000 women who turned up at both sites in 1982 to *Embrace the Base*. We surrounded the bases holding hands on the third anniversary of NATO's decision to store nuclear weapons in Britain. Between 1980 and 2000, over 70,000 women protested and it was the largest women's protest since women fought for the vote in the early 1900s. Women were arrested, fined and jailed if they failed to pay the fine, which happened to a friend, Nuala Young. The cost for the UK and US of fighting this protest was exorbitant. The attention it received was substantial, although I have to say little was positive in the mainstream media.

And the women won. The cruise missiles left in 1991 and the US Air Force followed in 1992. As the saying goes: *Nonetheless, she persisted.*

President Ronald Reagan and Prime Minister Margaret Thatcher embarked on an anti-Soviet and anti-Socialist crusade. Their speeches were full of the Manichean rhetoric: Us versus Them, Good versus Evil. People became frightened that a hot war could develop from the Cold War, as it was in the developing world, but with an additional nuclear threat because Reagan implied that cruise missiles could be fired in Europe. The government's response to people's concerns was to direct the Central Office of Information to produce a book called *Protect and Survive* on how to survive a nuclear attack. In effect you dived under a table.

Shirley's idea was to run a series of workshops with the teenagers. She suggested that they imagine being given the book at school and asked them how they would react. At the end of six weeks they produced the outline of a script which Shirley polished. We recruited a heavy metal band and produced *The Fall Out Room*. It was a success from the point of view of everyone who took part and the vast majority of the audiences. A few members did not feel the same way. They wrote to the new chairman saying that Shirley and I were as bad as the IRA as we were indoctrinating the children, even though the young people had devised it themselves. Rather than reacting to that, I came up with what I thought was a super idea: a healing and fun summer show. I should have left well enough alone.

I wrote a harmless revue called *Song of the Thames*. Some sketches and songs were written by KADS members, including an adapted nursery rhyme about 'toys for the boys' written by Shirley. The toys were not teddies but bombs, represented by balloons. It was too out there. David, the chairman, insisted that I not include Shirley's song. I wrote him a reply, which I thought was rather nice under the circumstances, extolling Shirley but pointing out that,

I could have brushed off those nasty comments comparing Shirley and myself with the National Front and IRA as ridiculously funny if they hadn't deeply hurt Shirley and contributed to the illness of a good friend. The nursery rhyme sketch you have taken offence to was meant to lessen the tension not increase it. The aim was to laugh at those ridiculous accusations. I don't agree with censorship so I'll keep it in the show and after it ends, I'll resign from KADS.

That was the end of my theatre career!

This may all seem storm-in-a-teacup. But grant me a moment. In the fifties, it was generally accepted that women were second-class citizens. The suffragettes had won the vote but not equal opportunities or equal pay. The first Women's Lib conference in the UK was held in Oxford in 1970. The new feminism spurred male-only colleges to admit their first female students in only 1974. It's worth considering that if, in 1981, it had been a man who'd written the songs, would the outcome have been the same?

Patriarchy has proved surprisingly resilient. I watched the rise of Donald Trump with his overt misogyny and his gloating about assaulting women, and was astonished. I'd thought we'd gone so far past that kind of man that he could never be elected.

That worries me. I'm the mother of men but the grandmother of women. In my own struggle for a world where people are judged not by their race or class or age or religion, they still seem to be judged by their sex. In my novels I make my female characters strong, intelligent and capable—like women really are.

Polly Biswas Gladwin's grandparents on her mother's side were from Iceland and I enjoyed the tumultuous stories from her first visit there alone, aged eighteen. This recipe is from her Icelandic heritage although she has great recipes from her English and Indian connections too.

Polly's recipe for <u>Auður's Icelandic Pancake</u>

Flour – half plain and half self-raising.

Enough eggs to mix until flour is incorporated–I always use a whisk.

Then add full fat milk until it feels like single cream.

Add vanilla pod or extract.

Add a dessert spoon full of caster sugar.

Add a couple of ounces of butter.

Leave to settle then put through a sieve to remove lumps.

Leave for a while.

Using a non-stick pan, oil the pan with butter, but not too much.

Cook the pancake on both sides, until they have stopped making a noise.

Serve with whipped double cream and strawberry jam – either roll the pancakes or fold into triangles.

CHAPTER 17: A Glass Ceiling and Scientific Racism

Atam fulfilled his dream of getting his PhD. His supportive head of department, Mr Pilling, approved a sabbatical in 1974 and Atam enrolled for his PHD at University College London's Galton Lab. His tutor, Cedric Smith, soon realised he had an exceptional student. Atam's specialisation was quantitative genetics.

A predecessor at UCL was the father of modern genetics, Ronald Fisher. He was regarded as a genius who almost single-handedly created the foundations for modern statistical science. Everyone in the field quoted and admired him. Like many geniuses he didn't write down every detail of his thinking. Many statisticians had tried and failed to complete the workings of Fisher's 1918 paper, which had led to many new areas of study. Atam succeeded and in the process discovered errors. These were important findings because of the way Fisher's work had come to be used.

Fisher's classical work, *The Genetical Theory of Natural Selection*, was a successor to Darwin's *The Origin of Species*, and became the basis for a whole new field of experimental and theoretical analysis in population genetics. Darwin's theory of survival of the fittest was either not understood or deliberately distorted by the eugenicists. Sometimes described as 'measuring heads', it was a fixation for many in the scientific community for a hundred years. Somehow it managed to prove the inferiority of women, working-class and black people's brains. Scientific racism got rebranded for the modern age by Arthur Jensen and Richard Herrnstein in the USA, and in the UK, by Hans Eysenck of Kings College and Richard Lynn of Ulster University who, as recently as 2006, published *Race Differences in Intelligence: An Evolutionary Analysis.* A previous publication of his was *Skin Color and Intelligence in African Americans.* That says it all!

President Nixon wanted an excuse to cut social programmes, like Sure Start begun by Kennedy and Johnson. If it was pointless teaching black people due to their genetic inability to grasp higher level learning, why waste money? In the UK, something similar had happened. The research of an influential psychologist of the heritability of IQ, Sir Cyril Burt, had justified the tripartite system of education, the three streams I described earlier: grammar, technical and comprehensive schooling. The system divided families and permitted the state to better fund the grammar schools as it was a waste of resources giving quality education to working-class children.

We met Professor Leon Kamin when he came to London while Atam was writing his PhD. Kamin had come in search of two women who were cited as responsible for collecting Burt's data on which his research and the consequent government policies were founded. They were Miss Howard and Miss Conway. Try as hard as he could by delving into the university records and asking people who had worked with or in close proximity to Sir Cyril Burt, Leon could find no trace of them or a single person who had met them. He eventually came to the conclusion that Burt had invented his data and that it was, therefore, no more reliable than 'measuring heads'. Kamin published his results in 1974. Burt had died three years earlier at the age of 88, celebrated to the end.

Atam was awarded his PhD in 1975 and his thesis was published in the prestigious peer-reviewed journal *Nature*, followed by two more papers published in *Nature* and others in the *American Journal of Psychology.* (See Reference Section)

Because of the interest, in 1979 he was the first Polytechnic lecturer to be invited to give a three-week lecture tour of the Ivy League universities. One of them was Princeton University, where Kamin was a professor, another was Harvard, where he caught up with Stephen Jay Gould, and a third was MIT where Adrian would read for his own PhD. Professor Jerry Hirsch, who believed that Arthur Jensen's scientific racism was a misuse and misrepresentation of behaviour genetics, had become a fan of Atam's research. They started to publish together. He described Atam's equations to me as 'elegant'.

One of the problems with genetic studies intended to classify races was that they usually used wrong formulae in their analyses so their results were worthless. Another major problem is that intelligent behaviour is controlled by the brain, but in the genetic analyses, the brain has no role. It was thought that a child is born with millions of neurons and no new neurons are created during a lifetime. Now we know that when a person, irrespective of age, learns something new, new neurons are created in the brain. Thus, an old dog can learn new tricks.

Because of the interest in his lectures, Atam was invited to take a sabbatical at the University of Chicago at Champaign-Urbana. It was the last thing Mr Pilling was able to arrange for Atam. When he retired, he took us aside and explained that because Atam had set up the degree course in Maths, Stats, and Computing in 1971, he had recommended him for promotion to principal lecturer. Mr Pilling looked sad as he told us that the other three creators of degree courses had been promoted. 'Only you were not approved by the Director.'

Subsequently, Atam organised a sandwich course, which involved placing students in industry in their middle year. It was hard work that involved travelling and convincing companies to accept his students for one year. He succeeded, so Mr Pilling again recommended him for promotion and again Dr Lloyd accepted the three other candidates and rejected one—Atam! Atam was the ONLY lecturer in Oxford Polytechnic who had set up BOTH a degree course AND a sandwich course and access courses for students who had not taken A levels.

Mr Pilling wished him luck saying, 'You are the only lecturer to tour the Ivy League and have papers published in *Nature* so I have recommended you for the new post of Reader.'

In May 1980, we set off for the States hoping that our worst fears were not true: that there was a glass ceiling for people of colour.

Recipe sent by my American/Canadian granddaughter Kerensa.

French Toast Supreme

Ingredients

Half cup butter

Two tablespoons of syrup or maple syrup

Two tablespoons of brown sugar

Slices of bread

5 eggs

1 teaspoonful vanilla

Quarter teaspoon salt

1cup evaporated milk

Method

Boil together the butter, syrup and brown sugar for 1 minute.

Grease 9X13 cm pan.

Pour the caramel mixture into the pan.

Put thick slices in the pan close together.

Beat the eggs, milk, vanilla and salt.

Pour the mixture over the top of the bread.

Cover and refrigerate overnight.

Bake at 325 degrees for 45 minutes.

When ready serve upside down.

CHAPTER 18: Insights into America

I loved American hospitality. The lack of snobbishness was attractive, as was the can-do attitude. The food culture is more diverse than the fast food chains, although that was when I first encountered McDonalds and one that interested me: Taco Bell. Nelson and Judy Kay Bard, who had taken their sabbatical in Kennington, took us to our first bring-and-share supper.

The conversation there was of the campaign to ratify the Equal Rights Amendment (ERA), a change to the constitution that would codify women's rights. There was more passion about feminism in the States than in the UK. In the seventies, Simonetta joined in the emerging women's movement but any spare time I could conjure was spent setting up the mother and toddler group, founding the theatre group (KADS) and organising events for my village's overseas aid organisation called accurately, if uncreatively, Kennington Overseas Aid (KOA). There is only so much energy anyone has to deal with the burdens life puts on us.

This American experience was game changing: it opened my eyes to the probability that I was more disadvantaged by being a woman than by being married to a man of colour. During this year, I realised that I hadn't read the iconic feminist books, so set about rectifying that.

Many of the women I met with Judy Kay were interested in training as lawyers to challenge gender inequality. These women were right about the importance of law. Married women couldn't own property in the UK until the Married Woman's Property act in 1882. Before that a single woman's wealth automatically transferred to her husband after marriage. Before the Equal Credit Opportunity Act of 1974 (yes, 1974), married women were not allowed to open sole bank accounts without the permission of their husbands. In 1966, Atam and I had opened a joint account.

After a week with the Bard family experiencing life in West Virginia, we headed south for North Carolina and Brevard where we stayed with Fopin's artist sister, Nachin, and her family. Her white American husband had built a delightful home on the edge of the Pisgah Forest about a twenty-minute drive from Asheville. The subtleties of language as a vehicle for culture were revealed to me in the States. 'Two peoples divided by a common language' was true. I was introduced to Nachin's husband, Randy, and wondered why he hadn't changed his name! It's short for Randal but the shortened version doesn't have the same connotations in the States.

Randy had a gun over the fireplace, another in his station wagon and one in his car. I asked why. He said, 'We're thirty minutes from the nearest police station.' As if that explained anything to me.

Nachin warned us not to stray onto the next-door neighbour's land. You couldn't miss the large signs saying TRESPASSERS KEEP OUT at the end of their drive but worryingly, there were no boundary fences. The neighbour was not keen on his Chinese-ancestry neighbours, and I guessed he'd have been no more enthusiastic about us.

After another week of sunshine, clean air, and generous hospitality of the Bones, we crossed Kentucky and eventually arrived in Champaign-Urbana. There was something chilled out about driving across America.

Jerry and Marge Hirsch gave us a warm welcome. They'd arranged for us to use a neighbour's house for three weeks. That house was how middle-class American life is portrayed in the movies: most of the gadgets in the kitchen were new to me, there was a vast basement with table tennis and other games, and I had my first experience of a tumble drier and, in the kitchen, of a waste disposal unit. That luxury was not to last—we moved into a part-furnished, two-bedroomed flat for the rest of the sabbatical.

We enrolled the boys in schools and their experience of US education was so good that it gave all three a love of the States. Novel for my football...oops 'soccer' loving sons, the under-12 league was co-ed. Why hadn't I challenged these gender social norms myself? Why had I grown up to accept them? I was unaware that when the game was created in England in the Victorian era, women's football was almost as popular as the men's game. The problem from the male perspective was that in the early 1920s some women's games were attracting crowds of 50,000 at a time when the men's game had not recovered from WWI. So what did the FA do? They banned women's football in FA grounds. With access only to muddy fields, the female clubs fizzled out.

As I write, my second son Adrian and his partner Juli are both keen players who encouraged their children, my North American grandchildren, Kerensa and Tristan, to love the game. I've enjoyed watching their prowess develop and Kerensa has been selected for a Quebec training squad.

Paul and Adrian went to Yankee Ridge Elementary School and Justin to Urbana Junior High, whose principal was black. The twin-town appeared well integrated so the story I tell now came as a big surprise to me. Atam invited two black professors to dinner: Professor James (Jim) D Anderson and a much older colleague, who had been given the opportunity to go to university after fighting in WW2. Our little flat was only part furnished. We had supplemented it with a few garage-sale purchases, so I felt I should apologise to them for the lack of elegance.

Their response shook me.

'You shouldn't apologise. You are the first white woman to invite us to dinner.'

Jim gave us a copy of a break-through just-published book, *Drylongso: A Self Portrait of Black America*. I came to understand how black people were rarely seen as individuals but instead were nearly always stereotyped. In the UK, people of colour faced prejudice but in the USA it was prejudice of a different sort, an altogether tougher league. The country had not and has not, even now, rid itself of the legacy of slavery.

Years later, an antiques dealer called Amanda Fore flipped through a copy of *Sculpting the Elephant* and read the dedication to anyone with a partner from a different country, religion, colour. She reacted emotionally and said, 'Glenn, my late husband, was African-American.' I understood his decision to settle in Oxfordshire rather than return to his home in Alabama.

Jerry Hirsch was of Jewish ancestry, and the famous playwright, Arthur Miller, was a cousin. I was keen to ask him about his illustrious relative but was disappointed to discover that they had met only once when Jerry was a teenager. Arthur Miller exposed prejudice and abuses of power in his plays, and Jerry wanted to expose both institutional and scientific racism. Atam and Jerry's first joint paper, published in 1977, was *The Misconceptions of Behavior Genetics* (University of Illinois at Champaign-Urbana). While they were working together during that sabbatical, Springer Verlag (a publishing company) suggested Atam and Jerry write a book together on the subject. I was delighted – this was a real step forward for Atam.

Before leaving for the USA, I'd been doing part-time teaching and DIY as well as catering for the boys and the three students living with us. I did everything domestic in the house and garden, while Atam concentrated on his career and publishing. I had a dream: a relaxing break in the USA. It didn't take me long to realise that, if I didn't work, I would meet no one. So on a trip to Chicago, while Atam took the boys to the science museum, I queued up with a variety of immigrants to get a green card to entitle me to work. I got a post as an assistant on the bi-lingual programme, a special class at Champaign High School.

The students learning English as their second language were immigrants from many countries but the largest group were Vietnamese—one of the outcomes of the war. The teacher in charge of the programme was called an 'instructor' and she didn't do any pastoral work and little bureaucracy. Her role was to teach. In the UK we expect far too much of our teachers. We want them to be social workers and relationship councillors as well as to teach.

Snow came early and Jerry and Marge gave us our first taste of Thanksgiving. It's good to remember how the first Americans saved the settlers but Angie Debo's *A History of the Indians of the United States* describes how they were rewarded with genocides and sustained warfare.

There is a campaign to talk about the British Empire in schools in order to understand why we have become a multicultural society. My generation learned about the voyage of the Mayflower and the struggle of those British colonists to survive, but not about what happened next. The stories I was told in school were of a benevolent civilising power, not about putting a price on Indian scalps.

The idea of emigrating to the States was mooted. Jerry believed a post for Atam at the University of Chicago was a real possibility. Atam's research was recognised and the evidence from US academia was that his career could thrive there. The boys were happy and I was adaptable. Despite loving Oxford, I was prepared to up sticks. Having married a man of colour meant my children were seen as mixed race. The least I could do for them was to make them my priority. My career decisions had to fit in with family life.

But I was glad when Atam decided not to apply for a post. He was influenced by what we had seen of the gun culture and drug problems which, at that time, were not so prevalent in the UK. He thought it would be better for the boys in Oxford.

Back to Oxford we headed.

Judy Kay Bard's Chilli, American Style

(Not a Texan, I can't vouch for a Texan's opinion of this...)

1 lb. hamburger (ground beef)
1 large onion, minced
29 oz., 822 g., can of tomato puree
2 15.5 oz., 439 g., cans of dark beans (black, kidney, red, just not white navy beans)
2 cups, 16 oz., 430 g., of water
Lots of chilli powder, maybe a teaspoon
Salt and pepper, generous amounts —The chilli powder makes it distinctive.
Brown the hamburger then add the diced onion. When these are browned, add the tomato puree, beans, and water. Now add the spices.
You will have a fairly watery dish. And now, you turn it into chilli.
Stir the mixture; turn the heat to low.
Return and stir the dish, maybe every 5-7 minutes.
Half an hour's simmering will probably please you.
This process continues until the dish has simmered to a thickness far beyond soup.
You will steam away most of the moisture. As it cooks down, the chilli blends throughout.
This creates the scent and taste that I call chilli. Not much help, I know. Yet if the ingredients retain distinct identity, you need to simmer it more.
This one teaspoon of chilli powder I guess should give you a mild dish. If you like more heat, just increase the amount.
(Increase the amount of chilli next time you cook the recipe - I don't think adding it later in the process would work well.)

Chilli really does have a reputation for heat. You want it as spicy as pleases you.

You could serve this with a side dish of warm cornbread if you want a deeply "American heritage." (And on the cornbread your guests could add butter and honey. This might make you feel like pioneers.)

CHAPTER 19: Discrimination and New Ventures

It's great travelling but often equally good to come home, enjoy the cloistered beauty of Oxford and view the Thames through fresh eyes. Our friend Don Newton picked us up from Heathrow. The M40 hadn't been built and he drove us home through Henley. I realised what I had missed about England was its patchwork of history and stories told in its architecture.

Our return was marred by shocking news. Not only had Atam not been made Reader but the post of principal lecturer, the one the recently retired Head of Department had proposed him for twice for his achievements, had been advertised without him being informed.

Atam had only a few days to apply but got it in. Inevitably, this meant that there was no candidate more qualified or more experienced that Dr Vetta. The new principal lecturer in biology was on the promotions committee. He insisted that Atam was the only applicant with scientific publications, and should be promoted. He told Atam how the director had used his power of veto when the committee had approved Atam's appointment. I found it hard to understand why the director preferred to leave the post unfilled rather than appoint Atam. A colleague explained, 'It isn't just that Atam is brown, it's because he's brown and active in the union.'

Race and class. It's a killer combo.

The Lecturer's Union thought it unfair to continually reject Atam against the recommendation of the appointments board, so the full-time officer sought a meeting with the director. He did not change his mind.

Atam was elected to the Council of the Royal Statistical Society with the largest vote ever recorded for any candidate. Because of that he attended an international conference in Spain. When he returned, there was a note in Oxford Polytechnic's weekly bulletin that the Deputy Director, Dr Tonge, has been elected unopposed to represent the Poly on the Education Committee. Atam was surprised as the rules stated that a two-week notice should be given for an election. Only one week had been given and that was while Atam was in Spain so the director thought he wouldn't know about it. Atam objected to the election. They had to rerun it with proper notice and Atam had himself nominated as a candidate. He beat Dr Tonge by a wide margin and became the Polytechnic's representative on the Oxfordshire Education Committee and its Further Education Committee.

Over the following three years, the Promotions Committee continued to recommend Atam for promotion and Dr Tonge, who had by then succeeded Dr Lloyd as director, continued to veto his promotion. The lecturer's union decided to lodge a complaint with the chairman of the governing body. As required, he set up a panel of five with himself as the chair to hear the complaint.

Two days before the hearing Atam was asked to see the registrar. He said, 'I thought he was going to offer me some compromise. But he said, I should withdraw my case because I was going to lose it, as the director will say that if the panel accepts my complaint, he will resign. I told him to tell the director he should not offer his resignation as the governing body might accept it.'

The panel's decision was that Atam should be promoted, and that the promotion should be dated back to the first rejection of recommendation by the current director.

Not long afterwards, Dr Tonge retired for health reasons, Oxford Polytechnic became Oxford Brookes University and Dr Clive Booth was appointed as its first director. He was different in his outlook to the previous two directors, and Atam respected him and enjoyed working with him.

Atam's focus and energy had gone into fighting the injustice in the only way he could: by getting elected to the governing body. Fighting institutional racism can be exhausting. In this case, it was just one man but he'd been the one at the top and had been given a veto. Atam had finally shattered the glass ceiling. The sad thing was that it meant his attention had been diverted so he hadn't the time to write the book for Springer Verlag and his research had suffered. That was to change but the circumstances of that change were unusual to say the least.

∞

I wanted to apply for a teaching post but there was a problem: none were to be had. When Justin entered the village school, there had been three classes per year. When I enrolled Paul (born in 1974), enrolment had halved. This was the reality all over the county. Oxfordshire County Council offered teachers over the age of fifty-five the opportunity to retire early, and moved superfluous staff into their posts. Although the term had not yet been invented, I'd just discovered GenX.

Because I born in 1945, I'm a boomer (born 1945-1960, or as late as 1965 depending on which data set you use). I married at a relatively young age (although not unusual for that era) and had children at a relatively young age and close together in age (again not unusually so for that era). So my children ended up being Xers (born 1960-1980). If you study demographics, that makes a difference. It impacts on access to housing, possibilities of promotion, popular media and so on. I have to admit that I struggle to see the impact that being an Xer has had on my children, to which they would undoubtedly reply: Ok boomer.

All that was available to me was supply teaching. Some schools treated us substitutes better than others. After six months, I chose to work in just two schools: Donnington Middle School and Iffley Mead Special School. Because it was harder for a special school to attract supply teachers, the staff welcomed me. The school was like a family because the children stayed from age five to sixteen. With the younger age groups the teacher had the support of a teaching assistant. That was brilliant because she knew all the routines. Supply teachers can run into trouble when the school gives them too little information. I recall once a pupil at another school asking to leave the classroom to help set up the dining hall. I had not even been given an accurate timetable, let alone these details, so had no idea if it was genuine or a prank.

In Iffley Mead, I taught older classes alone. On one occasion, a boy rolled on the floor and started screaming. The other children noticed my horrified expression and said, 'Take no notice, Miss. Trevor often does this.' It was close to break time so I decided to believe the children. The bell rang; Trevor jumped up and ran into the playground. In many staff rooms, a supply teacher would be made to feel uncomfortable talking about such an incident. But at Iffley Mead, I knew I wouldn't be judged. The head teacher suggested I do the special training and become a full-time teacher there.

I thought hard about it. I genuinely love children and teaching. Also, it was all I knew how to do professionally. But I realised that I lacked the patience to be a good special-needs teacher. And besides, something had shifted inside me. When I made my decision to be a teacher, I was a teenager who had barely left Luton. Now I was thirty-seven years old. I supposed that somewhere along the line, I'd changed.

What could I do? I'd been infected by the can-do attitude I'd witnessed in the USA. At that time, my friend, Gill Hedge, was working in the carpet department at Selfridges. She too wanted something different. We came up with a plan: Let's start a business together!

I had two ideas, both garnered in the US. One was Mexican fast-food. We had a vision of tacos, tortillas and burritos going down well with students. I later got to know Helen Peacocke who was *The*

Oxford Times food writer for twenty-five years. Early in her career, she'd managed The Kings Head in Woodstock and for lunch had served baked potatoes with twenty-one different fillings. My idea was similar: not twenty-one choices but eight different fillings with half of them, unusually for the time, vegetarian.

The lease on a shop in Jericho came on the market. We made a business plan and approached a bank for a loan. Given that our combined savings was £200, our homes were required as guarantee. Gill and I couldn't do that and later, we decided we'd made the right decision when a friend ran into trouble. He set up a science/engineering business that seemed to have a great future. When a Yugoslav client dropped out as a result of the break-up of that country, our friend's bank wouldn't support him until the next order in the pipeline came through. He borrowed on the family home and when another order was delayed, the house had to be sold to pay off the loan. Nowadays, there are angel investors, crowd funders and venture capital investors on the hunt for start-ups. In the 1980s, starting a business was higher risk.

My second idea: a flea-market.

We wasted no time. We recruited stallholders and planned to do the catering ourselves. The only investment needed for our business was the hall rental, advertising, printing and the outlay on the food. We found the perfect location in the Clarendon Press Centre in Walton Street in Jericho (Oxford). Idris Jones, the artist husband of KADS friend Shirley sketched a beaming sun for our logo. Jericho was starting to gentrify, and the quality bargains and curiosities in our busy market were exactly what people wanted. You can guess why, in my novel *Sculpting the Elephant*, I wanted Harry King's Deco-rators to be in Walton Street.

We felt we were onto something and organised markets in Kidlington, Witney and Didcot. As we expanded, Gill and I realised that many of the dealers were earning more than we were. Catering was hard work involving one day shopping, one day preparation and full-on serving on market day. Some friends took over the catering, and Gill and I shared a stall and shared profits from sales as well as profits from organising the events. I cut back on supply teaching in order to explore the local auctions for stock, and in 1984, stopped teaching altogether. Although I also ended my career in catering, I had the confidence to deliver a freshly cooked, three-course meal for sixty to a hundred people for the KOA social and gala events, with the help of a small but super team. (For more about that, see Chapter 27.)

Three years later came the big blow. The manager of the centre decided that what we were doing looked so easy that he could do it himself. After all, Gill and I were women and anything a woman can do a man can do better! He refused to let us book dates in 1985 because he was going to run the markets himself. We had little time to search for an alternative. A new venture had started in George Street. It was called Omni. The typically complicated Oxford ownership was later to have an impact on us.

The City Council owned the building and leased it to Nuffield College, which then sub-let it to a company called Strigreef. Strigreef acted like a landlord letting space under licence. We were too late to license the best locations in the building, so we rented the large basement beneath what is now a pizza restaurant. It could accommodate twenty-five dealers but it wasn't suitable to use every day because the only ventilation was keeping the door open! We named it the Oxford Antiques Omnibus because of its proximity to the bus station.

Out of curiosity, we went to see what the manager at the Clarenden Press Centre had achieved in our absence. It was a sad sight: only seven stalls selling jumble. It closed two months later for good. I wish I could say that women in business in Oxford were respected but the truth is the opposite.

While we continued to organise fairs, Gill and I realised we must trade seriously to earn a living, so started to trade independently. The best way to learn the trade was to develop an eye. On our doorstep was the world's first public museum, the Ashmolean. I could pop into the ceramics gallery and study examples from different periods. Most fellow dealers were generous in their advice and I began to accumulate books on subjects that interested me. The more auctions I viewed, the more I learned—almost unconsciously—by handling objects and looking at art. I started doing most of my buying in the West Country.

In 1983, Dad developed a heart condition and was admitted to hospital. He'd never been a hospital patient before. He discharged himself, and once home took out his ladders and began to prune a tree. Mum found him. The funeral in Teignmouth Methodist church was well attended. Mike and Fo had their first child, Zoe, in 1981 and it's lovely that we have photos of him with her. Mike and I suggested that Mum move our way but she loved Devon and didn't want to leave. The Teignmouth house and garden were too high maintenance for her alone, so she sold it and bought a semi-detached house in Dawlish.

From 1985, once a month I made a buying trip west. Mum didn't drive and it meant I could take her to the supermarket in Newton Abbott and on other errands as well as do business. Visiting auctions and antiques shops was a great way to explore the county. My favourite was Bearnes in Torquay, whose pink, domed auction rooms overlooked stunning gardens with views of the sea, across which had come many of the eastern items that attracted me.

Victorian and Edwardian furniture, art nouveau, Deco and textiles had been regarded as not old enough to be antique and hence were affordable. We had two textile dealers and were way ahead of the curve. Some years later I reviewed *Threads of Silver and Gold*, an exquisite exhibition of Japanese textiles at the Ashmolean. I soon got the difference. Why were these works precious and celebrated? They were made by men. Most British fine embroidery and textiles had been made by women so weren't valued.

Like our Clarendon Press market, our Oxford Antiques Omnibus was popular and busy. Gerald Dykes of Strigreef noticed the steady stream of customers. We were on a monthly licence agreement. We moved in paying £400 a month but every few months he raised our rent. By 1987, we were paying £11,000 per annum for the basement. To put it in context, at that time, the millionaire businessman, Robert Maxwell, leased Headington Hill Hall, an 18th manor house set in beautiful grounds overlooking the dreaming spires, for the same rent. We saw a four-story property on Broad Street to let for £12,000 a year and went to see the agent. The City Council was in charge, and we, wrongly, assumed they would be sympathetic. We showed their agent our accounts, so that he was aware that we could easily pay the rent. He turned up his nose and said, 'You do realise that if a financial institution is interested we won't consider ANTIQUE LADIES!'

We arrived back at Omni to find the licensees in shock. They explained to us that Nuffield College, who had the lease on the building, had taken our landlord, Gerald Dykes of Strigreef, to court. The story seemed unbelievable.

Unbeknown to us, Nuffield College had not approved Dykes buying Strigreef in the name of his seventeen-year-old son and thereby changing ownership of the holder of the sub-lease. It showed its displeasure by requesting Strigreef vacate the premises and not accepting rent from its seventeen-year-old new owner! The twelve hard working licensees trading in Omni knew nothing of this and instead we kept paying our ever increasing rent to Strigreef. News of the writ was the moment when we came to know the truth of our situation.

Solicitor's fees being what they are, Nuffield College decided to pay Dykes to leave. All twelve honest businesses letting space from him were given one month to get out of the building. Nuffield College in compensation offered us a rebate of one month's rent, in our case £1,000. I estimated that over the two and a half years Dykes would have earned about £200,000 from his company's honest licensees because Nuffield hadn't bothered to inform us about the unacceptability of Mr Dykes. Now he'd been given an added bonus. I asked to see the Bursar of Nuffield College but he wouldn't even see me. So I left a note with his secretary:

We are less than fifty yards from the college. Why didn't you confide in the licence holders and ask us to withhold rents? That way, you would have had Mr Dykes out long ago, saved yourselves a lot of money in solicitor's fees and paying him off and maybe could have acted with generosity by giving us time to relocate.

We had to suppress our anger because we were confronted with the need to save our business. But this was not to be the last time that we experienced Oxford as an unsupportive environment for small independent businesses.

The only photo of Gill and me in Oxford Antiques Omnibus.
(Photo taken by our art dealer Simon Hunter)

Gill's Danish Girl with a Veil

6oz fresh breadcrumbs

3oz brown sugar

2oz butter

1 1/2 lb cooking apples

Carton of whipped cream

2oz grated chocolate or chopped

Mix breadcrumbs and sugar with melted butter

Cook apples until mushy (sugar to taste?) With half a lemon.

Put alternate layers of apples and crumb mixture in a glass bowl. Top to be the crumb mix.

Whipped cream to the top and grated chocolate and nuts on top

Chill ...Completely calorie free, Haha!

CHAPTER 20: To the Jam Factory

I say with regret that being called 'antique ladies' in a derogatory way was not a one-off. The square mile at the heart of Oxford is mostly owned by the colleges and the city council. In 1987, only five properties were privately owned. The agents employed by the council and colleges liked to meet each other and interested parties at the Clarendon Club, at 121, The High. In 2013, it celebrated its 150th anniversary and reads like a who's who of the bosses of Oxford's old established businesses.

This was and to a lesser extent still is, a problem for women in business in Oxford—the club only allowed men to be members. As women, Gill and I were excluded. In the eighties, the influential Rotary Club and Freemasons were also men only. Being successful is not merely selling a product for an amount greater than its costs. Being part of the business community offers advantages and information that is impossible to replicate. I say that not from sour grapes, but from the perspective of an enterprising woman who was let down by that situation.

Why didn't we make a fuss? Life was too hectic coping with work, family, household duties and volunteer activities. Or maybe the discrimination seemed mild compared with what was happening in other parts of the world? I was involved in the Anti-Apartheid Movement. In the crowd in Hyde Park celebrating Nelson Mandela's birthday, while he was imprisoned on Robben Island, I knew my problems were luxuries. Gill and I accepted our exclusion and simply got on with the job of achieving within the sphere open to us. I'm not saying that's right or what women should do. I hope other women don't put up with that kind of nonsense but you can only fight so battles at any one time.

The battle we chose was for the survival of our business. Two properties came on the market in Park End Street opposite the station. Cooper's Oxford Marmalade Factory had been purpose-built in 1903 and after WW2 had been occupied and neglected by the County Council for twenty-five years.

The size of the Marmalade Factory and the modernisation it required put it way beyond our means, but a double-fronted shop at the opposite end of the row was well within our means so we pitched for it. Behind the shop was a courtyard with two flats to let. If we covered the courtyard area, we could accommodate our dealers and the income from the two flats would pay our expenses. It was perfect for us, except that Styles and Whitlock, Christ Church's agents, would not consider us for it. Nigel Braithwaite said, 'There's lots of interest in this property. Have you considered the Marmalade Factory?'

A publisher called Robert Norton wanted to move out of Wapping just as Rupert Murdoch was moving in. The unions, which had safeguarded well-paid working-class jobs, were under attack. Given that the print union ran a closed shop, I can't say I had much sympathy for them but the miners–that's another story. This was the pivotal time when the unions lost influence and greater inequality in the future became inevitable.

Robert Norton was attracted by Coopers Oxford Marmalade factory because of its proximity to Oxford Station but the problem was that he had no use for the ground floor. If the agents couldn't let the premises to Robert, they suspected it would take them a long time to find a tenant. And that was the reason the agents were keen to introduce us.

We immediately warmed to Robert. Robert's idea was that his own business would occupy the top two storeys and he'd convert the first floor for short term business lets. Among the occupants who would lease that space were two energetic young men who had just founded a business called Carphone Warehouse, award-winning local architects, Berman Guedes and a TEFL teacher.

Robert suggested we pay for the conversion and renovation of the ground floor and because of that, he'd expect only a small profit from us. Given my experience with Doreen (nee Walker) you'd have thought that I'd have got it in writing! We only had a month's notice at Omni and the shock and time pressure affected our judgement. I was so unused to professional relationships, having instead always operated on good-will, that I simply didn't know how integral contracts were to business.

Simonetta looked over the sublease for us and warned us against signing. The reason? No one in the building, not even Robert himself, was allowed to be under the Landlord and Tenants Act. To occupy space, we had to sign away those rights. Christ Church owned all the streets in that part of west Oxford. If a developer showed an interest in the entire area, the college could easily repossess the properties.

But we loved the building. From the moment we saw it, we nick-named it 'the Jam Factory,' because 'marmalade factory' didn't slip off the tongue. It was either sign on the dotted line or abandon the goodwill of our stallholders and loyal customers. Given the miniscule chances of two women being allowed on the first rung towards establishing a business in Oxford, it was this or nothing.

With the help of some of the dealers, we cut our costs as much as possible by doing DIY. Together we did the decorating, sanded and polished the floors and knocked down walls. Big expenses included installing lighting, the security system and the signage, constructing the Marmalade Cat café and extra loos. We attached 'The Jam Factory' logo over the side entrance and Oxford Antiques Centre around the front. Our name for the building has stuck but few people are aware of the origins.

Three months later we opened, although we very nearly didn't. A County Council planning official decided at the last minute that we would cause traffic jams and wanted us to be denied use of the building. *The Oxford Times* wrote about our dilemma as the *Traffic Jam Factory!* Common sense prevailed when we showed them the loading bay area between the two halves of the building and explained that not all thirty dealers would be in everyday, there would be rotas of dealers, and ten of them could carry their stock in bags on the Park and Ride!

What I sensed was a lack of trust in small businesses and that lack of support was a sign of things to come.

Using income from the licensee rents, it took us a year to finish the improvements to the rear of the building, buy plants and planters and purchase display cabinets. It was fourteen months before Gill and I could pay ourselves any salary, so we worked extra hard at trading.

All were welcomed: office workers, tourists, families with children, and the trans, who were into vintage fashion. They mixed with the likes of authors PD James and Brian Aldiss, and scientist Sir Richard Doll, who made the link between smoking and cancer. Desmond Morris, best known for his book *The Naked Ape*, collected Etruscan vases and thrilled us when he was accompanied by his friend, David Attenborough. David collected studio pottery but the most refined, for example Luci Rie and Hans Coper. I think he enjoyed the non-pretentious atmosphere. Our customers ranged from Romany to Princess Margaret. Oddly enough the Romanies didn't haggle much but Princess Margaret did. As our fame grew, we were used as a venue for TV shows, including one with Sister Wendy. A few characters in *Sculpting the Elephant* are inspired by real Jam Factory people.

1989: The Jam Factory when we occupied it

Tourists loved us so I took some of our leaflets to the Tourist Informa-
tion Centre. They refused to take them because we were 'commercial'.
I looked at everything else they were promoting: the hotels, the New
Theatre, The Oxford Story, even Blenheim Palace and the tour guides.
I said, 'None of them are charities.' Didn't get me anywhere!

We wrote to the City Solicitor and they finally agreed that this
was not a valid reason to exclude us. They said, however, it mustn't
be just about us, the leaflet had to be all antiques businesses. A new
regional association was proposed by William Clegg of the Country
Seat. We were among the founder members of The Thames Valley Art
and Antiques Dealers Association (TVADA). It produced an attractive

brochure which of course included the Jam Factory. I showed one to the manager of the TIC and she agreed that would be okay. Printing was expensive. A box of leaflets cost us £250, in 1990. I took them to the TIC. When I went to see how they were going, there was no sign of them. I asked at the desk and they pointed to the box behind them. When I asked why they weren't out on display, the manager replied, 'We'll give one to anyone who asks for one.'

I took the box away. A year later the City Council employed a City Centre Manager at an attractive salary. I wrote to him and explained that we had services available nowhere else in Oxford (rather like in the current TV programme the Repair Shop) and I'd love to show him around and talk through a few problems. He never came.

We started to organise regular events: Victorian, Edwardian, Swinging Twenties and Deco weekends etc. Anything to add to our visitors' enjoyment. And enjoy it they did, many making friends with our dealers. We became well known for our parties.

Me preparing for an Edwardian weekend.

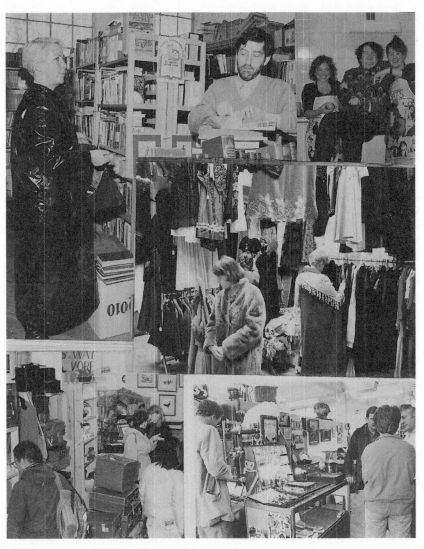

Collage of life in the Jam Factory

Atam and me celebrating our silver wedding anniversary

Despite the lack of council support, everything was going well and Gill and I looked forward to the company making a profit, now that we had paid off the bank loan and finished the work on the building. The devastating blow was that Robert Norton's business was in trouble as Robert struggled to make the transition to computers. Instead of informing those of us on subleases to see if we could jointly take over the head lease, it got offered to a property developer.

Unlike Robert, the new head lessor, Anthony Gresswell, the owner of Wellister Investments, didn't like what we were doing. The third-year break point in the lease with its rent review was due. Anthony wanted to double our rent. We showed him our accounts and said we'd have no choice but to leave. He relented and put it up by a third, which we had to pass on to our dealers. It meant that our limited company was only just in the black. Then gradually he increased our service charges from £8,000 per annum to £20,000, which was why we later looked for alternative premises.

Squeezing profit from us in the form of overpriced and invisible services may be perfectly reasonable from the perspective of the kind of capitalist whose only interest is in money, but it ensured that thirty tax-paying livelihoods were threatened. We have to recognise the weakness inherent in the most ruthless form of capitalism. In 2022, organisations working on a cooperative model like we did in the Jam Factory could be the way to bring life back to a struggling High Street.

The big plus for being self-employed is that I could be in control of my hours. Unlike so many working women, Gill and I could be there for our children on important occasions. Like many women (and hopefully an increasing number of men), the ability to integrate the needs of having a family with the needs of earning money required flexibility and cooperation. In that regard, the Jam Factory was as rare as hen's teeth. I knew it at the time. One of the reasons why I remain so fond of it is because it offered me something that I knew I couldn't find elsewhere. Career women will remain trapped or vulnerable to underpay or shunted aside until all parents, male and female, have more rights. The Jam Factory's method of cooperating for the general good was a good example. Our management style of caring about the people we worked with was not encouraged at that time. 'Good' management was ruthless and driven only by profit margins and to a large extent still is. For us, profit was not to be at the cost of human kindness. The atmosphere was like that of a family. We supported each other through tragedies and losses, including mine.

After a serious accident while converting a building to flats, my brother Ray's GP suggested he take early retirement. He had built and lived in beautiful houses but Ray and Jean decided to try out Dawlish as a possible retirement location and bought the Wimpy house next door to Mum. Ray extended it, added a conservatory and then left Jean to paint it while he went on a coach trip in Europe. I went to Devon every month and I was with Mum when he returned from that trip desperately ill. He was rushed to hospital, had eight pints of fluid taken off his lungs, was diagnosed with Mesothelioma and given nine months to live. The asbestos he'd handled as a young man in a dirty factory in Stoke-on-Trent (after he left the police force) had caused the cancer. He wanted to live what time was left to him to the full. When I was in Dawlish, he liked me taking him to country pubs and I enjoyed listening to his stories.

Seven months after the diagnosis, one Friday Atam said to me, 'You should go and see Ray.' How he knew I have no idea but I took his advice. Gill supported me so that I could have the weekend off. That was the last time I saw him. Given our fifteen-year difference, we had never been close, but I loved him dearly and I mourned his passing.

∞

We had a stand at the TVADA Fair in Eton College. It was interesting watching the horror and disbelief on the faces of our fellow exhibitors on Black Wednesday, 16 September 1992. That was the day when the British government was forced to withdraw the pound sterling from the European Exchange Rate Mechanism. This was before Brexit but with the benefit of hindsight, it was a portent.

∞

In 1990, Adrian was in his first year at LSE reading Maths and Economics and my sons preferred parent-free holidays. So Simonetta and I travelled together across France and Italy. I suggested we see Carmen in the arena at Verona—something she hadn't done before. The opera starts at 9pm but if you are in the cheapest seats, the *seconda gradinata*, you try to enter soon after the gates open at seven. Tickets were only £7 and you paid another £1 to hire a thick cushion to put on the stone steps and buy a candle. People had bought picnics and students plied us with sandwiches, 'impermeabiles' in case it rained and libretti. It was pure theatre before the show even started.

When the wealthier patrons entered to take their seats in the arena, the ladies around us kept a running commentary. I asked Simonetta to translate. They were a group of fifteen cleaning ladies from Mestre, near Venice. Can you imagine coachloads of cleaners going to the opera in England? They were commenting on the elegance, or lack of it, of the arriving guests. I recognised 'Bella donna Italiana', but sadly the lady wearing brogues was met with tut tuts of 'German' and that ugly mixture of colours? She had to be English. I found myself looking anxiously at what I was wearing. As it grew dark everyone lit their candles and floodlights lit up the villas on the hills—magical!

Moving the giant sets meant there was a thirty-minute break when you could go into the square for coffee or a drink. I became conscious of a man staring at Simonetta as she lit her pipe. She had recently appeared in a Sunday Times supplement in a feature about women who smoked pipes. The man looked familiar: it was Cecil Parkinson, one of Mrs Thatcher's favourite men, in Italy representing the British government at the FIFA World Cup.

Simonetta went on to become a famous novelist in Italy and has written recipe books and appeared in cookery shows on Italian TV. Here is one of her favourite desserts.

Simonetta's Almond cake without flour

Ingredients

300 grams almonds, ground with the whole skin, or very finely chopped
6 eggs, separating yolk from white
150 grams sugar
A small coffee spoon of ground cinnamon
a teaspoon of sherry or port or brandy (in Sicily we use marsala) optional

Method

Preheat oven to 160 C.

Grease a medium (23 cm) cake tin, add sugar to the tin, shake the tin and remove excess.(You can line it with baking paper and grease the paper). This will help later the removal of the baked cake from the tin, when it has cooled.

With an electric blender whisk the egg yolks with the sugar until smooth and without sugar grains. It should become pale yellow.

Whisk separately the egg whites until they form standing peaks.

Mix gently the whipped eggs into the whipped yolks, and then slowly and gently fold the almonds in the mixture. You can add drops - no more than a coffee spoon - of sherry, port or marsala.

Bake in the preheated oven for about 40 minutes.

When the cake has a light brown crust, check that it is ready by inserting a wooden skewer into it. If the skewer emerges dry, the cake is ready.

Leave the cake to cool in its tin, then carefully transfer it to a serving plate or tray, and dust it with a little ground cinnamon. It can be eaten at tea time or at dinner, with a fruit salad, and lasts for 2-3 days.

CHAPTER 21: Transitions for Atam and our Sons

In today's world, when retail takes place twenty-four hours a day, it's easy to forget that it wasn't always thus. It was only with the passing of the Sunday Trading Act in 1994 that shops could trade on Sundays. We closed the Jam Factory at 2pm on Christmas Eve and didn't reopen until January 4.

Justin graduated from UCL in 1990 and passed the fast-stream examination entry to the Civil Service. His first post was at the Treasury but with promotions, he moved to Education and Communities and Housing. As I write this, it has been renamed. It will be known as the Department of Levelling Up, Housing and Communities (DLUHC). There's politics for you!

Atam and I were trying in our own way to 'level-up' our children. We'd witnessed what a difference it made if a parent could help their child onto the property ladder. When you love your children, you want them to have a better life than you. The situation in the housing market is, and always has been, unfair. The interest rate soared and thousands of properties were being repossessed and auctioned. We had saved enough to put a deposit on a house for Justin. London prices were not like now. The house in Normand Road in West Kensington had been repossessed by a building society, boarded up and the meters removed.

Squatters had entered through the roof so there was a hole in the main bedroom ceiling. The squatters burned the lounge carpet for heat and the garden was piled high with black sacks filled with rubbish. We could see that this seventies house was basically sound so bid on it and were successful. Atam and I, with Justin, Adrian and Paul, and Justin's friends, set about making it liveable. We were even able to repair the damage to the roof ourselves, when we found the tiles that had been removed. We repaired the ceiling in the same manner we had in our own house at Upper Road.

While at university both Adrian and Paul lived some of the time with Justin but he let one room to help cover his overheads. Adrian graduated from LSE in 1994. His Head of Department, Bruce Shepherd, rang me. Bruce had been surprised that Adrian hadn't attended convocation because he was the Graduate of the Year and had won the Sheldon Prize—the joint maths prize for the whole of London University. Adrian told me when a football match had gone well so I couldn't understand why he hadn't told us about the Sheldon Prize. For my sake, when he received his MA, he went to receive it, with me to watch. My sons don't see their achievements as anything to go on about. Maybe they don't tell me because they suspect I'll boast about them—and of course, they'd be right.

Oxford Polytechnic, where Atam started his academic career, began life as the Oxford School of Art (and architecture) in 1865. In 1992 the polytechnic became a university. The founding principal of the school of art was John Brookes and they used his name in its new title: Oxford Brookes University. All ties with the local authority were cut. The new smaller governing body mostly consisted of businessmen. There was one representative elected by the non-teaching staff and the teaching staff elected Atam. He proposed Andrew Smith, the Labour MP for East Oxford, to be Chairman.

This transition from polytechnic to university was happening throughout England, driven by larger forces of globalisation. As our in-dustrial base shifted to other countries where regulations were lighter and labour was cheaper, the possibilities for a clever, hard-working youngster to rise through the ranks of the working class narrowed. My father's reality was long gone and with it, the pay cheque. Everyone knew it. The future lay not in manufactured production but in the service sector: well-paid working class jobs were disappearing. The service sector was to produce two thirds of our GDP: finance, education, law, consulting, the creatives, tourism, medicine and insurance. The only entrance was through education.

Over the next eighteen months, Atam realised that the new universities were going to be run as businesses. British students came with a fixed income. Extra money could be raised by building and letting accommodation, attracting foreign students and organising conferences. The governing body mostly focused on these business opportunities. Projects dear to Atam's heart, like the foundation courses for mature students and the ratio of staff to students, no longer mattered. The aim was to decrease the number of teaching staff and increase the number of administrators. To that end, some teaching staff were offered the opportunity for early retirement.

Atam had smashed the glass ceiling for minority and ethnic staff but it was his successors who benefitted. He wanted to take advantage of the chance to leave but was anxious about the drop in income. I suggested he make up the difference by trading at the Jam Factory, while he decided what he wanted to focus on. He wasn't the only trader with a PhD because Ged Ledger had a DPhil in Classics.

Atam joined the Jam Factory part time and found a new lease of intellectual life in research collaborations with French academics and published in French scientific journals and attended conferences in France. Without all his responsibilities at Oxford Brookes, he was able to enjoy thinking about how the brain works and publish on it. He still writes on topics like gene editing to this day. He adapted far better than I had expected.

We marked the transition with a trip to India for the wedding of our nephew, Rakesh, whose father Roshan had died young. We had named

Adrian, Adrian Roshan after him. We were so proud of the success his children had made of their lives. Atam had been their inspiration and he took on the role of head of the family. That meant that I was chosen to accompany the bride to her new home. I won't forget that emotional drive with Rama and there will always be a special place in my heart for her. Afterwards it felt as if Atam and I were on honeymoon as we stayed in romantic places in Rajastan.

These are Rama's recipes. I used her name for my female protagonist in Sculpting the Elephant but spelled it with a double MM.

Saag means - Sarso + bathua + spinach) leaves - 1kg + 250 gms + 250gms = 1.5kg (sarso - mustard leaves and bathua- special palak leaves)

Ginger- 2-3 small pieces or 1 big piece.

Garlic - 10-12 cloves - finely chopped

Tomatoes (in paste form) - 4 to 5

Onions chopped - 1 to 2

Corn mean (makki ka atta) - 2 tb spoons

Green chillies- 2-3 - finely chopped

Salt - as per taste

Clarified butter (Desi ghee) - 1 big spoonful

Method

Cut the leaves into small tiny pieces (if not already cut) and wash under plenty of running cold water.

Put the mixture of all the leaves along with green chillies + ginger + 3 to 4 cloves of garlic in a pressure cooker along with half glass of water - 10 mins on high heat and thereafter 20 mins on medium flame (Total - 30 mins) - or until it boils and is soft and mushy. Let the steam go off and let it cool. When it's okay to handle grind the mixture with a handheld grinder or on table top grinder in batches.

Put 2 tablespoons of cornmeal in the saag and let it boil for 10 mins - keep aside.

In a separate pan, (prepare TADKA)

3. Put in desi ghee (clarified butter) - let it heat for a while

4. Add the remaining garlic cloves - simmer for 2 mins

5. Add onions - simmer and add tomato paste

6. Add tadka into the saag and keep on low heat fr 15- 20 minutes

Serve hot with makki ki roti

MAKKI KI ROTI:

It is the best combination with saag in almost every Indian house, especially in the Punjab. Makki ka atta is yellow in colour. It requires a bit more effort and constant kneading to get a smooth consistency.

Cornmeal - 1cup

Lukewarm water - 1/2 cup

Take 1 cup of makki atta and add warm water (little by little) and knead it – until soft smooth dough is achieved.

Make tennis size ball of the dough and roll out on a disc and rolling pin with hands

Cook over a hot griddle on both sides till brown spots appear.

Put saag in the serving container. Garnish with hot ghee or butter and serve hot with hot rotis.

CHAPTER 22: Beginnings and Endings

Gap years are common in the twenty-first century. When Paul, my youngest, wanted one in 1992, they were rarer. They weren't organised like today and one that went wrong had led to the death of a friend's son, so I panicked. The internet had started but was not sophisticated like now. I learned about *A Year in Industry* from an old-fashioned leaflet. I gave it to Paul explaining that he didn't have to do it for twelve months as there were placements for eight months. He could earn money and then travel during the final four months. That's what he did. He was employed by Brent Chemicals in Slough, who made fluids for aircraft cleaning. When I asked him what he had learned he said, 'I don't want to work in industry!'

'Well, that was worthwhile then,' I replied.

With £8,000 in the bank he arrived in the USA to spend two months touring with two friends. Then he headed for India with Adrian to go trekking in the foothills of the Himalayas with Rakesh, visit family and see the country of his father's birth.

Like Justin, Paul went to UCL, choosing to read history and economics, in which I was able to share an interest. (For his MA he went to the LSE for European Studies.) He was elected president of Ramsay Hall of residence but in his second year he moved in with his brothers in Normand Road.

One year, Justin came to Oxford to celebrate May Morning, a traditional annual Oxford event, with some of his sixth form friends. Among his fellow sixth formers was Amita Chopra. Amita's parents, like Atam, were from the Punjab. When they moved to Oxford, they established the first Indian Restaurant in the Cowley Road. They named their restaurant *The Moonlight*. As students, award-winning novelist and poet Vikram Seth and cricketer turned Pakistani president, Imran Khan, headed there when they missed genuine Punjabi cooking.

When Justin brought Amita home to introduce her to us, Atam realised why. Amita's parents, Partap and Sneh, had had an arranged marriage and only knew arranged marriages. It wouldn't be possible for Justin and Amita to live together, or even to date for a long time. Like Atam and I, they had to decide quickly whether to marry young. Atam explained to me that we needed to visit her parents. We liked them immediately. Although Justin and Amita's was a love match, it made them and their extended family comfortable that we went through all the rituals: the Rookah when the close family members meet, the betrothal and the Indian wedding. It was a fabulous compromise between English and Indian practices.

On 13 March 1995, Paul turned twenty-one on the weekend of Justin and Amita's marriage, so it was hectic and delightful. We celebrated Paul's birthday at the Moonlight Tandoori on the Friday 10th. (Pratap and Sneh had sold the restaurant, hence its new name.) Vegetarian dishes had centre stage because, in 1988, there were four vegetarians in our family: Atam and Justin were joined by Paul and me. Over a few years I had reduced my consumption of meat. I asked myself, 'Could I kill an animal?' When the answer was 'no', I decided I couldn't expect others to do it for me. Nowadays vegetarianism and veganism are regarded as mainstream, and is even encouraged by the environmental movement, but that wasn't always the case. On a raining-cats-and-dogs holiday in Llandudno in 1982, looking for things to do, we attended the public lunch of the local vegetarian society. We met a delightful lady in her eighties who told us that when she decided to stop eating animals as a teenager she was treated as if she was insane and sent to a mental institution to be cured.

∞

Now lots of venues are licensed for weddings, but then you needed two ceremonies for Hindu, Muslim or Sikh marriages because a registry wedding was required to make it legal. The registry wedding was on the Saturday 11th, officiated by a KADs member, Jean Rowe. The official betrothal and lunch followed in a hall in Marston. In the evening, our extended family watched a film of Justin's stag weekend. After seeing that, I no longer felt sorry for him being expected to wear the Punjabi tinsel veil. The house was packed to the rafters. Staying with us were Mum, Mike and Fo and their children Zoe and Max, and niece Debbie over from the States. Paul brought Elizabeth Ludlow. (Their story could be the plot in a romantic novel.) Ray's daughter, Leslie, and family joined us while Jean, Angela and Steve stayed in a nearby B&B. Mum's surviving brothers and sisters, and Simonetta and her sister, Kiara, and Jam Factory friends and Atam's colleagues came on the day.

By Indian standards, the wedding was a modest 200 people. (Rama and Rakesh's in India had involved 500 people.) The groom's party was a paltry hundred. After the arrival of the groom's party and the gar-landing, tea, samosas and pakoras were served. Then the ceremony began, conducted in Sanskrit by Mr Kumar from Bicester. He had print-ed an English translation of the ceremony.

It was fun to see the difference between the way the 'Indian' guests behaved and the 'English'. The close family members sat on the stage where we helped create the fragrant sacred fire. While the English guests seated in the well watched intently, the 'Indian' guests walked around the upper area socialising as children played with balloons. For the final fifteen minutes, they too became quiet and attentive as Justin led Amita around the fire seven times and then she led him making their promises and garlanding each other. Then the feeding began. Two trays of ludoos (an orange coloured India sweet) were placed beside the bride and groom on their thrones and all family members came up to feed them a morsel as a way of welcoming them into the respective clans. Considering sweet food isn't a favourite of Justin's, he did well. Then all the friends joined in. Lots of silly bits of fun happen at Indian weddings. The bridesmaids hid Justin's shoes and would only return them when he gave them a big tip. The sit-down meal was followed by a touch of the West: the cutting of a British wedding cake followed by a disco, bhangra and bar.

March 1995 Justin and Amita's Wedding

Only the close family went to the Chopra's home for the Dolli and we bought Amita home to us. After their honeymoon in Goa, she went to live in Normand Road, London.

Justin's house had been dubbed 'Maison de Garcons' by Dr Christiane Capron, who collaborated on papers with Atam. Adrian and Paul were living there, and so was my college friend Annie Wright's son, Michael. Amita had grown up in a predominantly female household. Could she share her home with not only with her new husband but with three other men too? Would she cope? I was anxious and talked to Simonetta.

She said, 'Don't worry. If it's a problem the boys can stay with me in Dulwich.' Justin had lived with Simonetta for six months during his time at UCL, so she was being very generous. Adrian would soon fly the nest and head for MIT in Cambridge Massachusetts to do his PhD. It was going to be one of the worst times of upheaval for me.

We had just experienced the second break point in the lease at the Jam Factory and as I feared, our company would never be able to make a decent profit. The landlord was the beneficiary of our efforts. Our sublease would end in 1998. I suggested we keep our eye open for alternatives. A wonderful opportunity was on offer.

The Old School in Gloucester Green was owned by Oxford City Council. It was Grade 3 listed but, like the Jam Factory, had been neglected. The City Council wanted to move the Tourist Information Office there. The proposal was that the leaseholder must refurbish the building to a high standard in return for a 24-year lease at a peppercorn rent. We went to see the planner to check that what we had read was for real. The Council stated that its priority, after showing that we could restore the building, was a tenant who could bring life to the recently built square behind the bus station. I explained that that was us to a tee but we would be a consortium of small businesses, and a national or international hospitality chain could always outbid us. The survey and business plan would cost over £3,000 and that was a lot for us to waste. We were reassured that the statement was sincere. How gullible I still was!

The upper floor had huge slanting windows, making it the perfect location for an architect's firm. Berman Guedes also wanted to get out of the Jam Factory and they represented one third of the group who would bid. Atam had taken his pension partly in cash so that we could have two shares in the consortium and ditto for Gill and John. Dealers Paul Lipson and Sally Young were to be the other members. For once the bank was eager to lend to us. We were a perfect match because Berman Guedes was able to appoint and oversee the surveyor and Adkins, who would provide the business plan. That meant Gill, John and I could work on a programme to bring life to Gloucester Green. I won't go into the detail of our ideas—it's too depressing an exercise.

We dropped off the business plan and brochure at the planning department and waited. One evening, out of the blue, I received a telephone call from the West Oxford Councillor, John Power. He told me that the council had considered the Old School that afternoon but had not been given copies of our plan and our brochure, but merely told that, to move the Tourist Information Centre into the building, 'the antiques people' wanted £150,000 and Green King, the huge pub retailer and brewing company, expected a mere £75,000 from the council. There was no discussion and the vote went in favour of the catering giant. We should have been given notification and with it, the right to attend the meeting. Adkins had informed us that the formula they used was what all interested parties would use, with the same result. They were proved correct when, ten months later, The Oxford Times reported that Green King would be opening a pub in the Old School with the TIC being moved there at a cost of £145,000 to the council: they could hardly say £150,000 given the circumstances. To my knowledge, Green King never organised anything in Gloucester Green. I'll leave the reader to draw their own conclusions.

Meanwhile at the Jam Factory, the head lessor was negotiating the renewal of his lease for a further ten years. When that was agreed with Christ Church, he began to talk to us. With everything looking settled, it was time to sign on the dotted line.

We arrived one morning to find a letter giving us notice to quit! The CEO of Wellister Investments said he had changed his mind and wanted to turn the ground floor into a restaurant and conference centre. As Simonetta had pointed out, we had no rights because we were not under the Landlord and Tenants Act. All we could do was oppose planning permission. We petitioned the City Council, asking the planning authority to refuse this application. Over 3,000 customers signed it. But none of us was surprised when we lost and planning permission was granted. That was how my sixteen-year partnership with Gill ended and the Jam Factory family split asunder.

I struggled to understand the advantage to Wellister Investments Ltd. Once again *The Oxford Times* provided a credible explanation. Wellister Investments (WI) owned a golf course on Boars Hill. Anthony Gresswell's company had created the golf course, initially without planning permission. Was it surprising that after becoming a councillor, he received retrospective planning that came with two conditions? One was to create a nature reserve with public access, which was done well. The other condition was to limit the amount of earthmoving because of the sensitive Matthew Arnold's view of the city.

When Wellister Investments was negotiating with us, a service station was being constructed at nearby Wheatley. Planning stated it should be sunk into the hill and not built proud. That involved removing over 300,000 cubic meters of soil. The developers saved on landfill tax by paying a smaller but still significant amount to owners of sites, including the Hinksey Heights golf course, to take the waste on their land. *The Oxford Times* reported it because it involved a breach of the planning agreement for the golf course. Wellister Investments must have made an eye-watering profit in a short time. I concluded, perhaps wrongly, that the Jam Factory without us could be presented as a tax loss and have saved tens of thousands in capital gains tax? Whatever the company's motive, it was prepared to damage thirty sole traders' livelihoods by not renewing our sub-lease.

This goes to the hard truth that capitalism is not trickle DOWN but trickle UP. The kind of capitalism we're experiencing is fine if you already have capital but if you are young, bright and enterprising with little capital, it doesn't work. Our governance is, sadly, part of the problem as it answers to those who already have the capital and not to those who are coming up from the bottom. Add to that, the local press is a shadow of its former self when it comes to scrutinising local government, which means even more can now be hidden from view.

It appears to me that crony capitalism is even worse in the 2020s than it was in 1998. This means that we are less wealthy as a nation because the cream can't rise. Our economies are not as responsive and efficient. Capitalism cannot function as it's supposed to in a corrupt landscape. We accuse the developing world of corruption but from my experience, England is not without corruption although we're better at disguising it.

I'm an enthusiast for private enterprise, and the creativity and wealth creation which it generates. My brother Ray and I are examples of the hard work and commitment involved in building a business from scratch using limited savings. The businesses that Gill and I built were progressive, promoted a greener way of living, a caring community and offered services that were hard to find elsewhere. Instead of coming out with a profit from a popular business, Gill and I lost everything—through no fault of our own. I wouldn't have minded if we'd screwed up, or if the vagaries of fate had knocked us back.

It's hard to describe the disillusion and sense of betrayal that I felt.

Shaken to the core, I didn't know how to respond. I was, and to a degree still am, optimistic and a problem solver. But when the world seems without reasonable possibilities, it's hard to be realistic or solve any problems. I didn't know how to deal with my depression, and classically, didn't bother trying—because I was too depressed.

Simonetta and Atam stopped me from getting too lost. After all Atam had been through, his solution was to put the experience behind me and start again. It took some work to pull myself together but that's what I did. And having been in that pit of nihilism and despair, I have enormous sympathy for those who can't pull themselves out, who don't ever recover from enormous setbacks.

But if I hadn't, I wouldn't be writing this book because I wouldn't have become an author. I try to use storytelling as another way to make our world a better place.

Partap and Sneh Chopra's Moonlight recipe.

Matter Paneer (Peas Paneer)

Ingredients

3 tablespoons of sunflower oil
1 large onion chopped
1 teaspoon cumin seeds (jeera)
1 inch ginger chopped
Quarter tin of chopped tomatoes
1 teaspoon salt
Half teaspoon of chilli powder
1 teaspoon of garam masala
1 level tsp of turmeric (Haldi)
1 tablespoon of yoghurt
1 pack of paneer cubed, spiced and fried to prepare.
Frozen peas
One and a half mugs of water
Chopped coriander to garnish

Method

In a large saucepan or wok heat the oil and the cumin seeds.
Fry until sizzling and add onions and ginger (and optional garlic).
Fry until golden and add the tomatoes.

Add the salt, chilli, gram masala and turmeric.
Sauté until the oil separates.
Add the yoghurt and sauté for 5 minutes.
Now add cubes of paneer and the peas.
Stir and add the water.
Bring to the boil and simmer for approx. 15 minutes.
Garnish with chopped coriander.

CHAPTER 23: An Opportunity that Changed My Life

I learned that good can come out of apparent disasters. Rescue was to come in an unlikely place: Didcot. Chance plays such a role in our lives. I doubt I'd have a writing career if Atam hadn't taken a part of his pension as a lump sum with the intention of investing it in a property. When the Old School Gloucester Green fell through, we looked elsewhere. An old warehouse formerly used by Southern Electric on Didcot Broadway was on the market for £100,000. Didcot was then regarded as an undesirable location, despite the town boasting one of the most popular tourist attractions in Oxfordshire: Didcot Railway Centre, home of iconic steam engines and a location in many films. If big investors hadn't had that negative perception, we wouldn't have had a chance of buying the property. (This is no longer the case.)

It needed huge amounts of work to convert it into Didcot Antiques Centre, but you will have gathered that would not put us off. It was the best investment we ever made. Atam needed a large loan but in this case, the bank lent him £90,000 against the value of the property.

After our experiences in Oxford, I couldn't believe the encouragement we received from the town council. It had ambitions and appointed a friendly manager who regularly came and actually talked to us!

Will Clegg of Country Seat approached me. After nine years as chair of Thames Valley Art and Antiques Dealers Association (TVADA), Will wanted to stand down and he proposed me to replace him. I was flattered but wary. I thought it would be hard to get the long-established wealthier businesses behind me so I didn't immediately say yes. Atam encouraged me to accept. That was how for the next four years, I was chair of TVADA. How strange is life? If that hadn't have happened I probably wouldn't have a writing career and you wouldn't be reading this memoir.

Tim Metcalfe was at that time the deputy editor of Limited Edition, the colour supplement of The Oxford Times. Because I was chair of TVADA, he asked me if I knew someone who would take on the arts-and-antiques feature writing. I volunteered.

The first feature I wrote was TVADA related.

My first feature in Oxfordshire Limited Edition

I managed to get the organisation on board for the need for a recognised sign for Art and Antiques but I failed to get TVADA to adopt a new slogan: Antiques are Green. Recycling was just coming onto the radar but recycling uses energy. REUSE, which is what the antiques trade is about, is the most environmentally friendly activity. I was ahead of my time on that one.

As I gained confidence I pitched to other magazines. *The Antique Dealer* even paid me to write 'My View,' the easiest money I'd ever earned. It went out of business a few years later, and I hope that was not because of my forward-looking opinions!

∞

1997 was special. Alongside Justin, I watched Elysia slip into the world. I was surprised and moved when Amita asked me to be there. When Amber was born two years later, we looked after Elysia. We took her to the hospital two days later, to bring Amber home. She loved peering at her little sister in the plastic cot. A few hours later as Amber still lay on the settee in Normand Road, Elysia looked surprised that Amber was still there. But it wasn't long before she was devoted to her sister.

Nursery fees were so high in London that it made no sense for Amita to continue to work for the DSS, so she took a career break until they found a place in a local authority nursery. In the meantime, she joined us at Didcot trading in jewellery and brought Elysia with her. Amita still trades part time, calling herself Love that Jewellery. We went to auctions together and explored the Birmingham jewellery quarter and the rag market, when it wasn't selling rags! It was a lovely way to get to know her well.

Paul and his fellow student friends had painted the Didcot premises in National Trust colours as a summer holiday job and Fopin's niece, Debbie, from North Carolina, stayed with us for nine months and set up the café in the centre. Paul's recipe may well have been one Gill and I would've served if we had set up the Mexican Kitchen or if I had created the first veggie café in Oxford at the Old School Gloucester Green. Debbie put similar dishes on the menu at Didcot.

Paul's Black bean burrito

Can be served as a burrito or as a chilli with rice.

Ingredients:

2 tins of black beans (400g)
1 cup of sweetcorn
1 large carrot grated
5 - 10 slices Jalapenos chopped (2 tablespoons)
1 tin of tomatoes
1 diced courgette
1 red bell pepper diced
1 large onion
4 gloves of garlic chopped or crushed
1.5 teaspoons of paprika
1 teaspoon of coriander
1 teaspoon of cumin
1 teaspoon of salt
Chilli powder or Cayenne pepper to taste
Grated cheese optional
1 tablespoon of rapeseed oil

Instructions

Fry the oil, onion and garlic until the onion is soft.
Add all the spices and stir for 30 seconds.

Add the carrot, sweetcorn, courgette and bell pepper and sauté for about 5 mins.

Add the black beans, tomatoes and jalapenos and simmer for 5 to 10 mins.

Serve with rice or warm tortillas (30 seconds in microwave) and serve as a burrito with or without cheese.

CHAPTER 24: Flavours of the Good, the Bad and the Ugly

Moving Mum into a residential home in Teignmouth was one of the most distressing experiences of my life. The dementia had been mild at first but then she started falling regularly. After she lay on the floor for hours after dislocating her hip, it was clear that two daily home visits and meals on wheels were no longer enough. She had not pressed the alarm button I'd organised; the idea of her dying alone terrified me. A few years earlier, I'd tried to persuade her to move near us or in with us but she loved Devon and refused. Instead we visited her.

I felt so cruel putting her in a home. I couldn't believe it when three months later, everything changed and, in her mind, the residential home had become 'home'. In 2000, we celebrated her ninetieth birthday at Jean's house in Looe. It was a struggle to convince her to come with me to Cornwall but she did, and had a lovely time. Mum died in 2003: I was with her. It was so peaceful, a quiet outing of breath as her spirit departed her body. Having witnessed it, I don't think I'll fear death. I was shocked by my tears because I thought I had mourned Mum already as she had disappeared little by little.

When you reach seventy, as I did a few years ago, losses are inevitable. The most poignant is losing friends and family. After Mum and all her siblings died, it was clear that I was of the generation next in line. There came a point when I was relieved that most of the Oxford Castaways I interviewed for The Oxford Times were not over seventy, because, during the last few years, I attended the memorial services of Air Commodore Bob Martin, Charles Swaisland, Roger Bannister, Brian Aldiss, Colin Dexter and Bill Heine, whose home had a shark in its roof. Is death the final surprise shark attack?

∞

In 2000, we began to experience problems at Didcot Antiques Centre. Some dealers were moving and others were retiring. Having enough people to staff it every day became difficult. Attracting traders to a not-historical town was not easy. We had worked hard to attract customers from the neighbouring areas by mounting attractive events like jazz lunches, Valentine's evenings, Chinese New Year events etc. But there was a sense that the environment for small businesses was getting tougher. Changes in society were affecting the antiques trade. Some serious shoplifting was the last straw.

We had paid off the bank loan and Atam persuaded me that we needed to close the centre and let the premises. The dealers were sympathetic because Marilyn Williams and I offered to organise a regular fair at Oxford Brookes—which we did using the Mike Rhodes antiques logo. Atam, Amita and I concentrated on trading together under the banner of Vetta Decorative Arts. We exhibited at prestigious fairs including the NEC, Earls Court, Olympia and TVADA. I was able to utilise trading fairs in my novel, *Sculpting the Elephant.*

Most fiction draws on real-life experiences. In *Sculpting the Elephant,* my heroine Ramma is involved in a racist incident with a fictional celebrity at a fair. I expect most readers will take it as creative licence: highly unlikely but within my rights as a novelist.

I wish.

In April 2005, we had a stand at the Antiques for Everyone Fair at the National Exhibition Centre. Exhibitors will recognise the pattern

I describe in my novel, from setting up to leaving six days later. On arrival, all the talk was about the BBC filming the final part of a new series titled *Dealing With Dickinson*. The cameras had been following the two teams of three antiques enthusiasts over two months as, advised by Dickinson, they spent close to £50,000 buying antiques at fairs and auctions, having them cleaned and restored and finally attempting to resell them at a profit. There were cameras filming the stand constantly.

On the final day, Sunday April 3, rumours went around that they had not done well. Sundays were often quiet so we could take a close look around the fair and chat with other dealers. I went first. I passed the Dickinson stand and, in my eyes, it was all glitter and no substance.

When I returned to our stand, Atam said the latest rumour was that the stock on the Dickinson stand was going to be sold at a big discount. I told him not to bother; there was nothing on the stand to interest him. But husbands rarely take the advice of their wives. Atam immediately realised that what I had said was true. Dickinson came towards him and began a sales pitch. Atam replied by querying the idea behind the TV show. He said that he was still learning the trade after eleven years, so how did Dickinson expect to teach anyone in two months? This is how academics go through the world, asking awkward questions.

Atam returned to me in shock, literally, pale and hardly present. Eventually he told me what had happened.

'Dickinson began to push me and abuse me. He was shouting 'Fxxxing Paki bastard,' as he dragged me away from his stand. I thought he was going to beat me up, he was so angry. I freed my arm and began to walk in the other direction. He came after me. I was so shocked I didn't hear all his insults. Lots of dealers came to defend me. Some surrounded me while others stood between him and me.'

The following day there were reports in a Manchester paper and in the Sun. No one who knew Dr Atam Vetta could possibly believe that the former secretary of the Royal Statistical Society would say, 'You are robbing us,' let alone poke Dickinson in the chest. Yet that was what was reported.

There were not many ethnic minority dealers at the show so Atam was easy to identify. Newspapers got in touch with Atam, including the *Antiques Trade Gazette*. Dealers who had witnessed the incident wrote to the ATG supporting the account I have just written.

TV GURU DAVID'S BUST-UP

TV antiques guru David Dickinson had a furious bust-up with a dealer yesterday — captured on film by his BBC crew.

He was talking to camera when the man stormed up and **POKED** him in the chest.

The BBC said the dealer ranted at Dickinson, 64, and accused him of ruining the antiques business. The perma-tanned star was filming his new programme How To Make An Antique Dealer at a fair in Birmingham's NEC.

By DANNY BRIERLEY

A BBC spokesman said: "The guy started poking David in the chest and saying, 'You are robbing us'. David gave some verbals back."

Witnesses claim Dickinson *(right)* made a racist remark to the man, who appeared to be Asian. One trader at

the NEC said: "The guy called David a disgrace. David was ranting. There is a lot of bad feeling about him in the game because he is always having a go at us on TV."

The BBC said: "David refutes any allegations of racism or impropriety."

Article from The Sun about the David Dickinson incident

192

One of the witnesses, Eric Brittain, wrote this on 13 August 2005 just before the show was aired.

No doubt the NEC is delighted with the publicity they are currently receiving via the BBC's Dealing With Dickinson programme. However it will be interesting to see whether or not the programme includes footage of the final day when we were there to witness Mr Dickinson dealing with Atam Vetta.

The events were filmed. Atam wrote to the BBC to get the footage. A file load of correspondence passed between Atam and the BBC but the upshot was that they denied any responsibility and therefore could not share the footage. The programme had been made by Lion TV. He was told that his complaint and request must be sent to them. He wrote to Lion TV but they refused to give him the recording, so he wrote again to the BBC. (See Atam's email letter)

This battle was taking its toll on Atam; he was becoming depressed. He decided to take the correspondence to our MP, the Liberal Democrat, Evan Harris. Evan was shocked by what he heard and read, and eager to help Atam. He said, 'Leave it with me. I'll talk to the BBC.'

A year after the incident, we'd still heard nothing and I suspected that Lion TV destroyed the evidence. In the meantime, Clarion, who ran the fairs in the NEC, refused to let us have a stand. We had been trading at the NEC three times a year for six years and built up a following of good customers. We decided that we had no other option than to stop trading. I didn't have the energy to start over yet again. We closed Vetta Decorative Arts.

Most people in my generation had one career for a lifetime. The prediction for my grandchildren is that they will have to change careers and learn new skills throughout their lives. I have lived that kind of life, unwillingly and unexpectedly. I wish the endings had been less brutal. It was as if I've been in a perpetual cycle of life: creating a wave, riding its fleeting crest and then tumbling to a crashing end. It can be exhausting and terrifying.

Subj: Re: See ID 11966479 12050988
Date: 15/09/2005
To: info@bbc.co.uk

Dear Ms Wilson,
Thank you for your email (13 August). I am sorry that my letter to the BBC Chairman landed on your desk. The reason for writing to him was that I did not think that you would assist me further.

In your email of 13th August 2005, you repeat your view that I should deal directly with Lion TV. This, of course, I continue to do. Please try to understand that the information I seek from the BBC has **nothing to do with Lion TV. It is in the possession of the BBC alone**. I try to explain.

The likely sequence of events was:
1. Dealers heard Mr Dickinson abuse me racially and one of them got in touch with a reporter of The SUN.
2. The reporter might have thought that Mr Dickinson was running a BBC 'stall' at the NEC Fair (or the dealer might have mad this suggestion).
3. The BBC did not tell the reporter, as you keep on telling me, "go to Lion TV". Instead the BBC PR team got to work.
4. The BBC and Mr Dickinson concocted a story. The BBC press statement bears the hallmark of an expert PR team (although almost each sentence is false or needs elucidation).
5. The BBC then contacted the Sun reporter and gave him the statement.
6. The reporter asked questions and the BBC PR team replied to them. He put those replies in quotes.

Obviously, such a sequence would show up in BBC telephone records, emails or other records. To draft the statement the BBC team must have made notes when discussing the statement with Mr Dickinson. Notes of the conversation with the SUN reporter must also be in the BBC records.

I would like the BBC to supply me all notes and records associated with the issuing of the BBC statement. I suspect that the SUN reporter also has the record of his conversation with BBC. I have requested The SUN for those records.

I ask the BBC again to supply me all the information that it has on the incident and its PR team feeding false information to the SUN reporter, under the Freedom of Information Act.

Please do not tell me that as my name was not in the statement, no harm was done to me. As I said earlier, given the ethnic composition of dealers at the NEC, when racial abuse is mentioned, I am easily identified. Many dealers recognised me immediately. Even the Sun reporter was able to identify me for he telephoned me at home. I have also suffered financially.

I have found it difficult to get information from the BBC. Even little bits have to dragged out of the BBC. For example, I asked Mr Bains to tell me the time on 3rd April 2005 when the BBC statement was issued. He has not replied.

Yours sincerely,

Atam Vetta.

This time, Atam struggled to surface after the crash. Like my father, he could have achieved more but even so, he had done exceptionally well. To this day, his research is regularly cited because it is relevant.

I tried to help but there was nothing I could do. I had to look on and see him suffer. Abuse of any sort leaves scars and this incident, more than all the problems he had faced, left the deepest wounds. We overcame the prejudice we experienced in Smethwick and when his contract was not renewed, he was offered a better post. When the discrimination happened at Wednesbury, we moved on to Oxford. The Polytechnic's director's prejudice, evidenced by his constant use of his veto to stop Atam's promotion, was distressing but Atam could look back with pride knowing that he had changed things for the better.

But this set back was different. This orphan boy who had worked while he studied for an external degree had prided himself in his self-sufficiency and his ability to overcome difficulties. This time he felt more like a victim without redress and it stung.

This chapter doesn't deserve an illustration from my grandchildren to start it off, or a recipe to end it. The Food of Love is sadly missing.

CHAPTER 25: Everyone's Life is an Epic

There can be positive spin offs from the worst experiences. I closed my antiques business to pursue an ambition to write. I loved reading and had frequently written for fun, not just my over-the-top poetry but also am-dram productions. Despite feeling like an amateur, I dared to believe in my ability to communicate in words, encouraged by the kind responses to my features in Oxfordshire Limited Edition.

This was how my journey to becoming a freelance writer and novelist began. I wrote for more magazines. Beginning in 2001, it was my privilege to review exhibitions on behalf of The Oxford Times Weekend magazine. My first review was of the Armani at the Royal Academy. I watched with a wry smile while Norman Rosenthal introduced Georgio Armani. Rosenthal had said that there would be fashion at the RA 'over his dead body' but he looked pretty alive to me. Armani had given the RA a large donation, which I'm sure had nothing to do with the U-turn!

∞

You may recall that in 1965, my history lecturer, Donald Tranter, introduced me to Chinese history, which was unusual for the time. That new topic of study captivated me and, when Chairman Mao launched the

Cultural Revolution in 1966, I bought a copy of his *Little Red Book* and immersed myself in it. Six months later, disturbing footage of teachers being humiliated appeared on our news.

My interest in China continued through the years. As a dealer, I'd been attracted to Chinese arts and crafts. To earn a living, you had to sell. But I wish I could have kept some of the Imperial Chinese ceramics I'd traded, because now they'd provide a pension. I could only afford to keep things for the home that had been particularly good buys.

I reviewed major exhibitions in London but few made as strong an impression on me as the first one-man show by a living artist at the Ashmolean Museum. In 2005, Qu Leilei's *Everyone's Life is an Epic* consisted of twenty-one contemporary portraits. Each subject had been asked to describe his/her philosophy. Under his portrait, a homeless man called Andy had written, '*You are not a failure until you give up trying,*' and his chiselled features were surrounded by bold colour with the Chinese translation in calligraphy that was integral to the work. I kept returning to the show. One day I saw a homeless man in tears in front of that portrait.

I loved the profound humanity in these paintings. The artist's style combined East and West but the emotion was universal.

I guessed that the most epic life could be that of Qu Leilei himself so I asked the arts editor if I could write a profile feature. He agreed and I headed for Wimbledon to interview him.

Qu Leilei told me about his life in China: mass indoctrination into the cult of Chairman Mao, the Cultural Revolution and then the partial opening to new ideas after the death of Mao. Qu Leilei had been one of the founders of the first contemporary art movement there called the Stars, at a time when democracy activists, poets, writers and artists were brimming with ideas and hope. More by accident than intent, he and his colleagues, including Ai Weiwei, became dissidents. It's the time described as Beijing Spring in the 2021 documentary of the same name by Andrew Cohen.

In the UK, we don't expect an art exhibition to be closed by the police but that is what happened to the Stars unofficial exhibition in Beijing. The aggrieved artists were persuaded by democracy activists to march in protest to Tiananmen Square where they were intercepted by 300 uniformed police.

I asked the sculptor, Wang Keping, what he thought that morning in 1979, before they marched to Tiananmen Square under a banner that said, *In politics we want democracy and in art freedom.* 'I burned all my diaries, all my letters, anything with a name on because I didn't think I'd be coming back,' he replied.

Why had so few people in the West heard about them and their story? I'm not a China expert but because of my life long interest in the country, I considered myself somewhat well informed. Why hadn't I, of all people, heard about the Stars?

This working-class origin, white, English woman was determined to tell their story because no one else would. How crazy is that! I spent much of 2006-2009 interviewing eyewitnesses in depth, reading and visiting China to research. Leilei gave me permission to use his eye-witness accounts of tremendous events seen from close to the heart of power as background to the novel. I wanted it to be accessible to anyone who knew little or nothing about China. I applied to study for the diploma in creative writing at the University of Oxford and was accepted. Being awarded the diploma in the Sheldonian gave me the confidence that I could do it. Being a student made me feel young again. Many drafts later, Claret Press published *Brushstrokes in Time* in 2016.

Brushstrokes in Time is set in China and Berkeley, California. I chose Berkeley because I fell in love with the place when visiting Adrian and his partner, Juli Atherton. Adrian gained a place at MIT to read for his PhD in mathematics. Most of its PhD students were from overseas. MIT had ninety-five Nobel Prize winners, more than many countries. Talent is distributed throughout the peoples of the world, and MIT understands that and profits from it.

A group of friends took a trip to Montreal, Canada. Adrian and McGill physics grad, Juli Atherton, climbed up to the cross in Mount

Royal Park and became life partners. Not only did Ade and Juli love the great outdoors but both have a passion for 'soccer'.

In 2008, Juli not only did her post doc at the Berkeley but my granddaughter, Kerensa, was born in California and likes to call herself 'a California girl'. I was full of admiration for Juli doing both these at the same time-I couldn't have done it. She was appointed Associate Professor at McGill in the Medical Department and I was there in Ottawa to watch her be awarded the prize for the best PhD in statistics in Canada that year.

We launched *Brushstrokes in Time* in Blackwell's in 2016, and I spoke in the Blackwell marquee at the Oxford Literary Festival. After I finished, a young American woman of mixed ancestry bought a book for me to sign. She looked as if she had been crying. She said, 'My mother came to the USA from China in the early nineties. Like your character Sara asking her mother, I asked mine to tell me her story but she refused every time saying, "Don't ask me. I want to put all that behind me." I understand but it makes me feel that I don't know her.'

I had got it right emotionally and also historically. John Gittings, the chief foreign correspondent of the Guardian had been in Beijing during those years, tried hard to find fault—but failed. And endorsed it thus: 'Vetta is always accurate with a grasp of vivid detail.' One of the best endorsements came from Shrenik Rao, the editor of the Madras Courier who has published some of my features: 'A brilliant, compelling read.'

To be a published author earning royalties with an upcoming London publisher, to have my work turned into an audiobook and translated into German were beyond my wildest dreams. As I watched the 5* reviews accumulate and read moving comments by readers I'd never met, it was hard to believe this was happening to me. As the story spreads and as other people learn of it through Andy Cohen's new film Beijing Spring, the world will discover the true story of talented and courageous young men and women who risked their lives for freedom of expression. *Brushstrokes in Time*, like the Stars' intentions, concerns love and hope against the odds.

This is an immodest brag. My apologies. It felt all the sweeter for being unexpected, all the more cherished after recent crushing difficulties in business.

There was something ironic about receiving the news that sales of the audiobook of *Brushstrokes in Time* and its chances of republishing with a bigger publisher were hit by criticisms of cultural appropriation on the same day that Liu Xiaobo, the dissident put under house arrest for agitating for freedom of speech and other civil liberties, died. Liu appears briefly in my novel in the chapter on the events in Tiananmen Square in 1989. To even mention that in China puts a Chinese person in danger, which is why a Chinese writer couldn't have written *Brushstrokes in Time*. I couldn't and wouldn't have written *Brushstrokes in Time* without interviewing Chinese people who had grown up during those years or been involved with the Stars Art Movement. My novel emerged into a strange world in which a one-party state imprisons dissidents while a 'progressive' West denies anyone else telling their thoroughly researched story, endorsed by Chinese activists themselves.

Researching for Brushstrokes in Time in Beijing with Leilei's mother, Lu Bo, who inspired Little Winter's mother and her daughter-in-law, the artist Caroline Qu.

Caroline and Leilei's Easy Peasy Pepper Chicken

Ingredients

One large chicken breast
Three peppers of different colours
Lemon juice – third of a lemon
One onion
Four garlic cloves
Four sliced mushrooms
Two cups of rice preferably Thai rice.
Two tablespoons of Chinese oyster sauce

Method

Finely slice the chicken into strips similar to spaghetti width.
(Caroline and Leilei say that slow is fast when cutting!)
Mix in the oyster sauce and lemon juice.
Rinse out the rice in its saucepan and finally add the same amount of water as the rice. i.e. 50% rice 50% water. Bring to the boil, turn down the heat and cover it.
Finely slice the onion and crush the garlic.
Add all the ingredients together and fry in a wok for 2 minutes and serve with the rice.

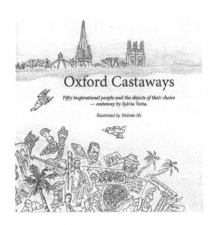

Oxford Castaways

Fifty inspirational people and the objects of their choice — castaway by Sylvia Vetta.

Illustrated by Weimin He

CHAPTER 26: Oxtopia

I was writing a monthly feature for the award-winning colour supplement of The Oxford Times. After collecting the National Press Award for the best regional colour supplement five years in a row, the editor didn't enter it the next year to give others a chance.

Each month for three years, I wrote on a unique topic. By 2001, I found that hard to sustain and suggested that I write a series. I called my first series the Antiques Time Machine and, starting with Gothic, worked through the centuries to the present. I shone a light on what people had in their homes during each era and what you could still buy from that period. The past is another country. When you hold something from another time and place, even a spoon, it can transport you there. Why do we say someone was born with a silver spoon in their mouth, meaning they are privileged? In Tudor times, when you were invited to dinner, you took your own cutlery. The poor ate with wooden spoons. The upwardly mobile yeomen used pewter but, when a wealthier child was christened, he/she would be given a silver spoon.

When I give talks on antiques or organise antiques quizzes for charity, I take button hooks. For me they sum up the constraints put upon female lives over the centuries. In the Victorian and Edwardian eras middle class women wore whale-bone corsets, which made it hard to bend. Boots and gaiters came with many buttons. If you were not wealthy enough to have a maid, how could you undo them? Someone invented the button hook! I take a skirt lift too and ask if anyone knows what it is. For me, it represents female liberation. With the invention of the bicycle, women could travel more freely but there was a problem; long skirts got tangled in the wheels, hence the need for a skirt-lift.

When that series ended, I moved to *Ask the Experts*. As well as the usual categories like art, furniture, ceramics, silver, jewellery and books, I reflected changing interests and included specialists in vintage fashion, costume jewellery, door furniture, telephones, ephemera, toys, teddy bears, curiosities from other continents and much more. When that series ended two years later, I was a more confident writer and felt I could embark on a project closer to my heart: *Every Antique tells a Story*. I began with a story of a pair of damaged vases I'd bought from a house clearer for £15. The C17th/ early C18th story behind the vases is a thriller; it's a tale of political intrigue, alchemy and kidnapping. Porcelain was the most desirable commodity of the seventeenth century. All over Europe attempts were made to copy the amazing Chinese invention. My vases, while not Chinese, were trying to be. They were a failed attempt to make porcelain by a Dutchman who pompously called himself Petrus van Marum. His 'soft paste' version copied a Chinese shape and design. These vases connect the dots in my own story. I love art, history and storytelling, and my first novel was set in China but I am not Chinese. These vases represent all of them.

I'd have loved to continue the series but some stories, like that of the apple scoops, were just a bit on the short side. Apple scoops are curiosities which take us back to a different reality. The English notoriously had bad teeth. If you lost your teeth, eating apples was nigh impossible without one to scrape small pieces. This is what they looked like.

Carved wooden apple scoop

Some friends at the Ashmolean Museum loved the series and even the director, Christopher Brown, had seen it. Two years later, he commissioned Theo Chalmers to take fabulous photos of celebrities holding an object from the museum telling its story. Those exhibition photographs were put on the back of buses and on the forecourt, while the museum was closed for the rebuilding work. In 2010, Christopher's friend, Neil MacGregor, shared my way of thinking with *A History of the World in 100 Objects*. He had the wealth of the British Museum at his fingertips whereas I just had my readers' stories.

In 2007, Christopher Brown was to prove important in my next series: *Oxford Castaways*. It was Desert Island Discs without the music. I invented an island called Oxtopia and suggested that interesting people from Oxford's Town, Gown and County be sent there with inspirational art, objects, and books. Having the world's first public museum in the city, it was a no-brainer to ask Christopher Brown if he would be my guinea pig. Because he said yes, getting other people to take part became easy. Even Chris Patten, the Chancellor of Oxford University and last governor of Hong Kong, and Shami Chakrabarti, when she was Chancellor of Oxford Brookes, agreed to be cast on Oxtopia. I also cast away the creator of the Headington Shark which has echoed through my narrative. John Buckley is an under-celebrated artist. He was working as a war artist for the Land Mines Advisory Group when it was awarded the Nobel Peace Prize jointly with another landmines charity.

When the fiftieth castaway landed on the island, my editor, Tim Metcalfe, with the help of artist Weimin He, combined the fifty interviews into a beautifully illustrated book called *Oxford Castaways*. Those fifty were joined by forty equally remarkable people and their life stories in *Oxford Castaways 2*, published in support of Vale House, the first hospice for terminal mental illnesses like Alzheimer's. The final castaway book, *Oxford Castaways 3*, was published in 2017 and proceeds went to Sobell House Hospice, thanks to castaway Dwina Gibb, who paid the printing costs. The seemingly infinite pool of diversity ended in November 2016 when all freelance writers were sacked by Newsquest, owned by the US company, Gannett. The Oxford Times is now a thin tabloid with little original content. The decimation of the local press is a national tragedy. The editor chose the final Oxtopian. The tables were turned as my life story ended the ten-year series.

The Oxford Castaway series enriched my life because I became friends with many of the Oxtopians and they turned the island into a kind of club, connecting people across careers and classes. All the Oxtopians were achievers but were modest with it. The advantage of approaching an interview without preconceptions was that I was constantly surprised by the stories I heard. I told the castaways that I would share the copy with them and that they were welcome to delete anything or add to it. That was why they felt they could trust me and were willing to reveal themselves. For example, Sir Roger Bannister, the famous runner, told me a story, not then in the public realm, of how he used himself as a guinea pig in an experiment on heart disease.

Like my own life, their stories intersected race, class and gender and were international. The 120 castaways were from five continents. Just one example among so many: Icolyn Smith was an inspirational example of how the Windrush generation responded to prejudice with love, not hate. When her husband died young, Icolyn took on three jobs to keep her family afloat. Despite having no savings she started the

Cowley Road Soup Kitchen, which mainly feeds homeless white men. She knew hardship and prejudice. She once rescued a little white boy who was about to run in front of a car, but his mother shouted at her, 'Get your filthy black hands off my boy.' I used her to inspire a character with her name in *Not so Black and White*.

The Manchurian-born castaway and former artist-in-residence at the Ashmolean and the Radcliffe Observatory Quarter, Weimin He, has sketched many events that I have organised and has illustrated many of my books. We have become friends and he sketched the launch of 'Stealing Dylan from Woodstock' by Ray Foulk, which I compered. I met Ray on a screenwriting course and was keen to cast him away on Oxtopia. In 1969, Ray and his brothers stole Bob Dylan away from Woodstock to the most unlikely location of the Isle of Wight. The Beatles and those festivals blasted through the class-ridden, patronising, conservative norm of the UK I knew as a child.

Weimin He's sketch of the launch of Ray Foulk's Stealing Dylan from Woodstock which I compered.

While writing the features, I had a blinding revelation, a vision of this amazing city of Oxford. It was not just the stunning architecture, the museums, libraries, theatres, parks, meadows and rivers but the PEOPLE, like Icolyn, John, Weimin and Ray, building their lives within this environment—people whose origins are from all over the world.

The final Oxford Castaway picture and one of the last events attended by Sir Roger Bannister. The compere was his daughter, the Right Rev Charlotte Bannister Parker (9 March 2017)

Some of the castaways at the Maths Institute. Sir Roger Bannister is in the middle. Back row from left: Korky Paul, Dr. Diana Sanders, Bill Heine, Annie Sloan (the chalk paint lady), Richard O. Smith (comedy writer), Joanna Harrison (Going on a Bear Hunt director etc), Philip Hind (film-maker), Dr. Chris Wright (Bio-chemist and supporter of young science start-ups), Nancy Mudenyo Hunt, Rev. Charlotte Bannister Parker, Professor James Leonard, Professor John Dewey, Prof Jim Bennett (Museum of the History of Science).

Front Row, Francesca Kay (author), Ray Foulk, Brigit Hegarty (designer), Dwina Gibb (artist, poet and playwright), behind Roger is Legs Larry Smith of the Bonzo Dog Doodah Band, Dr Yasmin Robson (Guyanan born astrophysicist), Gillian Cox (founder of the first hospice for people with terminal Alzheimer's), Trevor Cowlett, Icolyn Smith,

Dr Christopher Watson (who saved the world from a possible nuclear tragedy), and next to me Sister Frances Domenica (founder of the first hospice for children). Behind Christopher is the crossword compiler Don Manley, aka Duck, Quixote etc and some Sobell House hospice castaways.

Helen Peacocke was the food writer of the Oxford Times for 25 years and was one of my castaways; I used her recipes in *Green Power: The Spirulina Cookbook*. Here is a simple favourite of mine. A tasty way of serving kale.

Kale Crisps

Kale is not the easiest vegetable to cook. If it is underdone it becomes chewy, cook it too much and it can be come soggy. Bake it gently, however, in a moderate oven and it takes on a glorious crunchy finish that can be enjoyed as a finger food, or used as a garnish.

4oz (100g) kale Vegetable oil

1 tsp spirulina Sea salt to season

Wash the kale thoroughly and dry until all water has been removed from its leaves. Chop the kale into small pieces, removing the stalks as you do so.

Turn the oven to 325°F/170°C/gas mark 3.

Place the kale into a plastic bag, and drip in a couple of tablespoons oil. Shake vigorously until the leaves are all lightly coated with the oil.

Tip the kale onto a flat baking tray, and scatter with the spirulina and salt to season. Place into the middle if the oven and bake for about 10 minutes until nice and crunchy, checking after 5 minutes to ensure that the kale is not overcooked.

Spoon out onto kitchen paper when it has become crisp and allow to cool.

Place in an attractive dish and serve as part of a buffet, as a garnish or starter.

CHAPTER 27: Past is Future

We are struggling with the enormous change that's underway. These changes are not necessarily good or bad, they just are. They include artificial intelligence, globalisation, climate change and a subject Atam is currently writing about, gene editing. What's obvious to absolutely everyone is that the old ways are dead. But what's coming to replace it, human progress or modernised forms of personality politics and fascism? In my country, compassion and welcome for refugees is coming under attack. Despite my overt desire for us to see each person as unique rather than a representative of a race or class or ethnicity or demographic or fill-in-the-blank, I know that exhorting people to be nice won't get us to where we want to be. Can people change?

This had been churning over in my mind, occasionally at the forefront but mostly muttering away at the back. For all the positive changes, I could see an equal amount of inertia. I could hear the resistance coming at me from all sorts of quarters. Who were we to be if we were no longer permitted to be the way we were? How were we to organise ourselves for this new globalised reality?

I didn't know either.

Ironically, I found the answer in the past. When reading about ancient Indian history, I stumbled across another poorly known story, another Beijing Spring moment. It felt like the most spectacular un-covering of lost history. If I asked who founded Buddhism, I expect the answer would be Buddha. But that's rather like assuming Jesus founded Christianity. Jesus lived and died a Jew. (It was St Paul who separated Christianity from Judaism.) Similarly, the Buddha was a Vedic teacher in North Eastern India who attracted a large following but didn't him-self create a new religion.

The leader who founded the religion we know as Buddhism and who spread it across Asia started off as a notorious warlord known as Ashoka. Ashoka began as a typical ruler of his time (304BCE- 232BCE) and became more so as he extended his territory and his power. The bloodletting to attain victory at the battle for Kalinga changed his life and attitude. His remorse over the suffering caused was sincere, and he took instruction from followers of the Buddha. Although he contin-ued to rule in a secular manner, for the rest of his forty-year reign he tried to govern with Buddhist ethics.

The usual means of communication was by word of mouth, which could be distorted—relevant in these times of fake news. Ashoka promoted his new vision through rock edicts, that is, his words were carved on stone. Because the population was illiterate, he sent his emissaries all over India to read the rock edicts to the people. Here is one of them, Rock Edict V111.

> Thus of all the people who were slain, done to death, or carried away captive in Kalinga, if the hundredth or the thousandth part were to suffer again the same fate, it would now be matter of regret to King Ashoka....For King Ashoka desires that all animate things should have security, self-control, peace of mind and joyousness.

He renounced violence and desired that his government be informed by Dhamma, which can be interpreted as righteousness. He did not rule out self-defence but urged his descendants to value Dhamma over conquest.

As a warlord, his prison in Pataliputra had been a vile place and the converted Ashoka turned his attention to reform. He abolished the death penalty, ordered prisoners be unfettered and offered regular amnesties and employed ex-prisoners in his palace. He created a kind of welfare state, and even recommended the protection of wild animals—an idea two thousand years of ahead of his time. He advised against praising your own religion or denigrating a neighbour's beliefs. He disapproved of the caste system and preferred practical action to rituals.

Ashoka founded the world's first international university at Nalanda. It later spread over nine kilometres and had a huge library and 10,000 students. Circa 1193CE, Mohammed Bakhtiya invaded North India and not only did he burn it down, but he destroyed all the books and murdered all the custodians of that knowledge. One monk travelling with one book survived.

Earlier, the Buddhist explorer Xuanzang (602-664 CE) took 650 books from Nalanda to China. The Great Wild Goose Pagoda was built to house them. Thanks to him those books were later translated—and just in time. In 1966, Mao and Lin Biao urged Chinese teenagers to 'destroy the old.' People obeyed and burned books, including Daoist works of art and Buddhist books.

Ashoka's daughter persuaded her father to let her spread the teaching of the Buddha beyond India. She went to Sri Lanka and knowledge, via the universities and diplomats, spread into China. Between the two of them, the religion we know as Buddhism was born.

After Ashoka died, fanatical Brahmin rulers began the obliteration of his ideas and the memory of him. The language of Brahmi died out so no one could translate the rock edicts and Ashoka was forgotten for over 1,000 years. How could the founder of the world's third largest religion be forgotten? The world is filled with untold stories particularly of women and the losers in battles but I asked myself, 'Could this be the most significant forgetting in human history?'

What I most love about the teachings of the Buddha, Ashoka,

Jesus, Desmond Tutu and his friend, the Dalai Lama, is their emphasis on compassion. In a world in desperate need of good governance, in a time of enormous flux, I wanted more people to know Ashoka's story. I especially wanted to emphasise the possibility that people can change. There are better informed people out there who could do a better job of it than me. But if **no one else** is doing it, then I'm prepared to give it a go.

I was able to combine a research trip to North East India in search of Ashoka and the Buddha, with a family wedding in Mumbai—a lovely modern wedding because Ankita is Hindu with Buddhist attitudes and Manvir is a Sikh. It wasn't an arranged marriage. There were both Hindu and Sikh rituals over the three days. That seemed appropriate to the task of writing *Sculpting the Elephant*, about Ashoka and our new reality of negotiated boundaries of nationality, culture, religion, colour and class. All three of my novels explore mixed relationships like my own, which will be more common in the future, a reality that white nationalists in the mould of Enoch Powell, regard with horror. This novel brought together important strands of my life: the world of art and antiques, the search for a better way of living together, the utter necessity to recognise our shared humanity.

A photo that I took of the ancient university of Nalanda. Only one kilometre of the ruins has so far been uncovered. .

Once the novel was nearing publication, I visited the restaurant/bar at the Jam Factory, as it is a location in the novel. I asked Andrew Norton who runs it if Anthony Gresswell, the CEO of Wellister Investments was still the head lessor. After being told that he wasn't, I felt that a launch there could be therapeutic. The Jam Factory launch accommodated people from my trading past, some castaways, journalists and friends. It felt like one of those memorable Jam Factory parties with a difference; I'd moved on and put that past behind me.

At another launch, my granddaughters Antonia, Alexandra and Anastasia Vetta stole the show by playing the piano to an appreciative audience.

Weimin He sketched some of my family and the performers.

My granddaughters Elysia and Amber's recipe

Chocolate Brownies (They are lovers of chocolate)

Ingredients

185g butter
185g dark chocolate
85g flour
40g cocoa powder
50g chocolate (white or milk for chocolate chips)
3 eggs
275g caster sugar

Method

Melt butter and chocolate together in a bowl and mix.

Sieve plain flour and cocoa powder into a bowl.

Break 3 large eggs into a large bowl and tip in golden caster sugar. With an electric mixer on maximum speed, whisk the eggs and sugar. This can take about 5 minutes

Pour the cooled chocolate mixture over the eggy mousse and gently fold together with a spatula.

Add in the flour and cocoa powder. And mix together.

Finally, chop up some chocolate chips and add in to the mixture.

Add to a dish lined with baking paper and cook at 180 degrees for 25 mins.

CHAPTER 28: Life is Not So Black and White

In 1968, the Kennington churches invited people of all faiths and atheists to explore new ideas. Those meetings resulted in the founding of two organisations: Kennington Good Neighbours offers sympathetic and pragmatic help, especially the elderly. The other organisation was Kennington Overseas Aid (KOA), which eventually raised over £500,000 for development projects all over the world. That's quite an achievement for a not-wealthy village.

Whether we like it or not, what happens in other parts of the world affects us all: a butterfly flaps its wings in Africa and changes our weather. You can choose to ignore it or you can choose to engage with that. We chose to engage. This earth will only survive if everyone thrives.

KOA's chairmen had always been men who mostly served for four years. After six years leading the fundraising organisation, Tony Hillier was desperate to resign. He came to the Jam Factory and over coffee in the Marmalade Cat asked if I would take over. I'd been organising the main social event for many years. Indeed my first dramatic production was a one act play by Chekhov for KOA. Downhill ever since?

I sympathised with Tony but didn't believe I could fit the role into my life. He looked so disappointed that I said, 'I've an idea. Why don't I be the vice-chair and shadow you for a year and see if I can do it?'

A happy man, he went on holiday to Egypt. While there, he tragically suffered a heart attack which killed him. I was thrown in at the deep end. A few years into the role in 1998, I persuaded a reluctant (at first) KOA to stop supporting the big guys of development, but instead to approach smaller grassroots charities. That is how organisations like the Nasio Trust (founded by castaway Nancy Mudenyo Hunt), Tools for Self-Reliance, Lunch4Learning, Standing Voice and The Children's Radio Foundation (whose president was Charlotte Bannister Parker), benefited from KOA support. Our focus was on projects that helped people to help themselves. The result of the connection with small, often recently founded charities, was more feedback, closer ties and outstandingly successful projects. A further bonus was that we could introduce charities to each other. For example, bringing together the Nasio Trust and the Children's Radio Foundation resulted in a project involving Wallingford School in which castaway, Bill Heine, accompanied them to Kenya and broadcast daily bulletins on regional TV.

KOA was a good example of duality. It was an umbrella under which people of all backgrounds and ages united to enjoy events (some of which raised so little money that it wasn't about the money at all but about community building) and do something unselfish at the same time. It wasn't just good for the world; KOA was good for Kennington.

Of my involvement, many remember me more for the entertainment and food than for my role as chairwoman. Every year for twenty years, a small team helped me prepare a three-course meal for 60-100. The food was memorably good so it was never a problem selling tickets! It was the nearest I came to achieving that old ambition of a career in food.

KOA ended in 2018, when it celebrated its golden anniversary. When I had been chair for ten years, I too was desperate to resign. I came up with the idea of a triumvirate, which worked well for a further twelve years. One year you were chair and the next you had a sabbatical and the third you returned as vice-chair. At first it was easy to replace a chairperson who dropped out, but when Dr. Halcyon Leonard and I wanted to retire in 2016, there was no one willing to replace us. Two former chairwomen, Marilyn Farr and Brenda Groth, presided over 2017 together, to nudge us to the golden year. Halcyon and I oversaw a delightful swan song.

Because of my work in the community over forty-five years, the founding chairwoman of KADS (1978), the first Parent and Toddler group in Oxfordshire (1973), helping save the library (2012), but mostly for organising local events for KOA every year for forty years, I was given in 2018, the unsung hero award by the Lord High Sheriff, a dynamic woman called Jane Cranston. Her successor, Richard Venables, not only opened our final fun run but he ran it!

KOA's final event: a Golden Gala Night. I'm at the front holding the mike.

I've witnessed many beginnings and endings—possibly more than most people. Because of that experience, I have learned the importance of *good* endings. Because KOA made it to fifty, we were able to celebrate.

You could say that my life has been one long series of failures because all my careers have been cut short. Although Newsquest freelancers like me were sacked in 2018, Jaine Blackman let me bring the ten years of *Oxford Castaways* to a close in a good way; I can think of it without regrets. If you have to bring something in your life to an end, even if you don't want to, doing it well makes all the difference.

The abrupt endings of our Walton Street market, Oxford Antiques Omnibus, Oxford Antiques Centre and Vetta Decorative Arts feel different. All those endings were unexpected, unprepared for and brutal—like a shark landing in a roof.

Making the best of what opportunities come your way enriches life. Because of my almost life-long involvement in KOA, I produced five books! The first was *Oxfordshire Rambles*, the second *Green Power: the Spirulina Cook Book* (for the Nasio Trust) and the third was, *I Love You All*, a history of Kennington Choir. The choir was KOA's most successful fundraiser. I did it because the choir founder and KOA honorary life president, Trevor Cowlett, asked me. What comes of saying 'Yes? A year's work!'

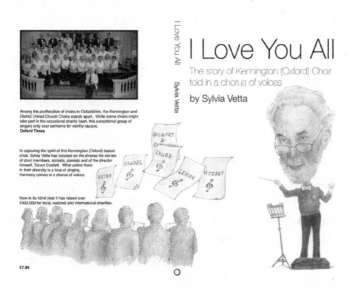

The cover of I Love You All (2015)

The fourth, *Poems in an Exhibition*, was for a relatively new charity: Standing Voice, which supports persecuted people with albinism in Tanzania and elsewhere. In February 2017, the BBC broadcast a documentary about Standing Voice titled *Born Too White*, which showed the clinic KOA had funded, so I had to watch it!

Halfway through this moving film we were introduced to Festo. Aged seven, Festo was mutilated with a machete because he has albinism. His teeth and fingers were taken for sale to a witch doctor. When the film was made Festo was nine and an inspiration. Using his remaining thumb and a piece of nifty surgery creating one finger, he'd become a talented artist. I told his story to my artist friend, Weimin He. We decided to send art materials to Festo and his friends, and Weimin wrote a beautiful letter 'from one artist to another' and sent Festo a painting especially for him. That painting inspired me to write a poem about it and to produce *Poems in an Exhibition* as a personal fundraiser to support an art summer school for Festo and his friends.

This story shows that the prejudice and fear that comes from 'othering' people is not only white—it's human.

My fifth and final book related to KOA was the novel *Not So Black and White*. Every decade of our lives has light and shade, sweet and sour. Don't be afraid of reaching seventy. It's generally recognised that when you are old, you rarely care what others think and can utter what you believe is the truth. If you remain open and interested, you can even make new friends. That's what happened to me.

In 2014, I met Nancy Mudenyo Hunt, who started Nasio Trust. KOA raised £25,000 to fund the building of forty tanks to produce a food supplement called *spirulina*. It's an algae that is 65% protein and rich in iron and other minerals. A little added to the diet of the over 400 orphans Nasio supports helps even children with HIV grow well. The idea was to produce enough extra to make it a commercial enterprise so that Nasio needed less donor aid.

The story of the Nasio Trust is bound up with the story of its Kenyan-born founder, Nancy Mudenyo Hunt. An experience of a racist incident not handled well by the police led her to apply for the post as a diversity trainer with the Thames Valley Police. Interviewed at the height of Black Lives Matter campaign, she said, 'It is about the systematic racism young people face, which I have seen first-hand when I accompanied them to court. The treatment of young people based on the colour of their skin could be absolutely shocking.' She resigned from it with reluctance but, once the decision was made, set about growing the Nasio Trust with fierce determination. Nancy would make an incredible business woman: her energies are transformational.

As we walked to her car after sharing a lunch one day, she said, 'Sylvia, I'd like to write a book with you.' I thought she meant a non-fiction book but that week, Claret Press had suggested that I write a novella and self-publish it on Amazon to help with promotion. Claret Press generously offered to edit and prepare it for publication for free. I replied to Nancy, 'Would you like to write a novel with me?'

Together we wrote a story inspired and informed by her life and what it means to be a girl in rural Kenya. We titled our novel *Not So Black and White*. It's a rare achievement because few novels are written by two unrelated people. Somehow we did it and readers tell us that it doesn't read as if it was written by two people.

You can be inspired by the contemporary relationships, female empowerment and personal transformations but I wanted one other aspect to be told in the voice of Precious's father, the local chief who, like Nancy's own father, attended the coronation in 1953. Not long after that, on 30 Sep 1955, Barbara Castle MP, later a cabinet minister in the government of Harold Wilson, wrote in Tribune magazine,

In the heart of the British Empire there is a police state where the rule of law has broken down, where murder and torture of Africans by Europeans goes unpunished and where authorities pledged to enforce justice regularly connive at its violation.

Duncan McPherson, later the head of ABC Corps, told Barbara Castle that conditions in the Kenyan concentration camps were worse than he had experienced in a Japanese prisoner of war camp.

Most Brits are completely ignorant of the atrocities committed in Kenya. They know about those carried out by the Mao Mao on white settlers, but not about the estimated 100,000 black Kenyans who died in the camps. The colonial government destroyed records of the concentration camps when Kenya became independent. It's a minor feature in *Not So Black and White* but we have the heroine's uncle return from one, a broken man.

How can we understand each other if we don't listen to each other's experiences? That, to me, is the point of the novel. Indeed, it's the whole point of reading. It's about inhabiting another's skin. It's a way of creating empathy and understanding because you walk in someone else's shoes.

Publication was planned for 1 June 2020. On 25 May, in Minneapolis, police officers illegally killed George Floyd, a 46-year-old black man, who had passed a counterfeit $20 bill. According to Statistica.com, between 2017 and 2021, US police killed an average of 227 black people each year, versus 421 white people. Numbers can be deceiving because only 13% (which includes people of mixed race) of the US population is black and 72% is white.

The Black Lives Matter movement had wings. All over the world, including here in Oxford, people of every colour took to the streets. The Oxford Mail and Times reviewed our novel, and gave it the caption, 'The book to read after the Black Lives Matter protests.'

Nancy and I were stunned by the coincidence of how the issues we had explored were so relevant. At one of the protests in Bristol in 2020, the crowd toppled the statue of the slave trader, Edward Colston. Bristol was built on profits from the slave trade and is home to one of the oldest black communities in the UK. Many Bristolians knew that they could have had ancestors on one of Colston's ships. Since the eighties there'd been a campaign to have at least a plaque describing how he made his money on the pedestal. We should know of his philanthropy to his home city. But we should also be aware of how he made his immense wealth and the cost in human lives. That campaign was ignored for forty years. Was that a case of black lives not mattering?

We are reluctant to tell the whole story; we cherry pick our history to make it sweet and digestible. It's a human trait—not just British. That's why we ignore the British Gulag in Kenya, the death of three million Indians in the Bengal famine in 1943 and a further million Indians because of how we handled partition. Partition alone caused more deaths than all the British and Empire casualties in WW2. We will become genuinely one nation when we can embrace all our stories. Knowledge, empathy and community: together they can beat the forces of oppression.

Recipe

Margaret Newton was one of my first friends in Kennington. She brought her son to the Toddler Group and joined KADS. For twenty years she cooked with me for the KOA gala nights. Margaret says, 'I mentioned to a friend, who was a KOA supporter and also happened to be a classical archaeologist, that I wanted an imaginative recipe for a KOA Gala Night. She told me about this apricot ragout and gave me a copy of Flower and Rosenbaum's 'The Roman Cookery Book: a critical translation of the Art of Cooking by Apicius.' As soon as I had tried out the recipe, it became my favourite food and it went down well at KOA dinners.'

RAGOUT WITH APRICOTS

MINUTAL EX PRAECOQUIS *from the Ancient Roman recipe book by APICIUS*

The original recipe gives no quantities, and some ingredients would now be very hard to get. Here is my version of the ingredients, scaled to using 1kg of meat.

1kg diced pork shoulder (I brown it in the olive oil first)

Shallots or 2 medium onions, chopped

Liquamen (fish sauce). I use 2tbsp Thai fish sauce, (be careful, it is very salty)

½ bottle wine (you could use less and add water as necessary)

2tsp cumin seeds

1tsp pepper corns

Dried mint

Dill

2tbsp honey

2tbsp wine vinegar

Passum. 3tbsp dessert wine (I use Masala if I have it)

Stoned apricots. I use 225g dried apricots, (perhaps cut in half) pre-soaked in hot water.

Tracta. Crumbled pastry, to thicken sauce at the end. Apicius tells us to use it, but I just use cornflour mixed with a little cold water to thicken the sauce if necessary.

Apicius's Recipe

Put in the saucepan oil, some fish sauce, wine, chopped dry shallots; add diced shoulder of pork cooked previously. When all this is cooked pound (in a mortar) pepper, cumin, dried mint, and dill, moisten with honey, (some more) fish sauce, dessert wine, a little vinegar, and mix well. Add the stoned apricots.

Bring to the boil, and let it boil until done. Crumble pastry to bind. Sprinkle with pepper and serve.

I like to simmer this slowly for about 2 hours, preferably in pans that will go in the oven, and I add more fish sauce or water if necessary. You end up with the most wonderful blend of flavours and aromas—sweet and sour, salty, umami, and nothing fishy about it at all. It goes well with good bread and most people will never have tasted anything like it.

CHAPTER 29: The Underestimated Importance of Libraries

I began this memoir with the story of a seven-year-old girl who fell in love with books when she entered a library full of them. The realisation that she could borrow any one from that treasure trove of knowledge and imagination, opened the world to her.

You wouldn't be reading this if I had failed my 11+. I tracked down a fellow pupil from Hart Lane Junior School. He's now a Professor at St Andrews. He also passed and it opened doors for him too. Our school must have got something right, but I believe that developing a love of reading was the key that unlocked a parallel universe for me.

Michael Rosen, the famous children's author, was the curator of stories at the Story Museum when I cast him away on Oxtopia. He told me that the evidence from everywhere in the world is that children who read for pleasure, do well academically. They find a lifelong friend in books. My story is evidence of the role they play in social mobility for kids whose parents can't afford to buy books. My community's library is small but it has access to two million books, provides free research facilities and free internet and is a busy community space which welcomes everyone as equals. The cost of running our library for a year was a mere £23,000. It's amazing value for money.

In December 2010, we received unbelievable news. As part of the austerity cuts caused by the 2008 financial crisis, twenty Oxfordshire libraries were to close, all in villages or suburbs without a surplus of amenities. The council's plan was to spend a little more on the larger town libraries and encourage old people and mothers to get on buses with their pushchairs and children and take an hour there and back. Really? Could the men and women who run this country have so little grasp of how the real world works?

Much has been written about the 2008 financial collapse of the banking sector, and I'll leave it to my betters to explain why and how a deregulated mortgage market in the USA caused a global financial meltdown. In the UK, the Conservative-Liberal Democratic coalition government decided that the best way to resolve this crisis was by massive state cutbacks across all sectors. There was, at the time, substantial economic data from twenty plus years of neoliberalism implemented in other countries, namely Latin America, that it didn't work at all. Neoliberal polices impoverished a people who were already suffering, reduced socio-economic mobility (unlike libraries) and transferred assets upwards.

I felt angry.

I contacted Reg Little, the reporter on The Oxford Times. Reg asked if a librarian would talk to him. I asked our library manager, my friend Dominique Henderson. The librarians were under threat if they spoke to the press but she agreed on the condition that her identity wasn't revealed. Thanks to her, the news of our campaign to oppose the closure was on the front page of the paper the next day. Parish Councillor and library supporter Paddy Landau and I met to discuss what to do. We set up the Save Oxfordshire Libraries Campaign to make sure we spoke and acted as one. My gut feeling was that would not be enough. The politicians and civil servants would easily outmanoeuvre us on their territory. We needed to find a way to outmanoeuvre their out-manoeuvring.

Oxford Castaway, Korky Paul, the illustrator of the popular children's books featuring Winnie the Witch, was popular at St Swithun's school so I rang him and asked, 'Would you lead our Pied Piper Procession?' He agreed.

On Monday 7 February 2011 at 3.30pm, a procession 300 yards long snaked its way through the village to share tea with the leader of the council. The children carried posters and noisy musical instruments. Korky wore his Winnie socks and followed Phil Freizinger, a flautist. The regional TV and the press filmed in the packed hall. I didn't allow political speeches. The adults gave the leader of the council, Keith Mitchell, 600 letters and a petition, the children their letters and posters. Then we allowed him to speak. But... he then had to sit and listen as Korky and MG Harris read to awed youngsters and interested adults, and to the children's choir sing:

'Consider yourself At Home. Consider yourself one of the family.'

The crowd filled the stage behind Keith and spilled out into the foyer and beyond. Keith had expected maybe fifty or so voters but what he got was a packed gathering where the youngest was a baby and the oldest was the former chair of FOKL and KOA, the castaway Charles Swaisland, aged 92.

Two days later, Keith Mitchell announced a rethink. None of Oxfordshire's forty-three libraries would close. When it comes to protests, take a page from novelists: *show not tell.*

We thanked Korky by making him our honorary life president. I asked him again if he would be a patron of our Build a Library campaign for the Nasio Trust. I'd suggested to Nancy that we donate some copies of *Not So Black and White* to libraries in west Kenya. There was a problem. In Mumias West, an area the size of Oxfordshire, there is not one library, neither in the community nor in schools. So we have set about raising the money to rectify that.

When Korky Paul comes to talk to the children of Kennington, our library manager, French citizen Dominique knows how to thank Korky: with a box of her madeleines.

Madeleines Recipe by Dominique Henderson

Madeleines are easy to make, you just need time! I advise to start the day before you wish to enjoy them.

Ingredients

2 large eggs or 3 medium size.

100g caster sugar,

100g plain flour

1teaspoon baking powder a must have!

100g unsalted butter- Very soft, like a hand cream or melted but cool.

Optional;

Flavouring such as 1 teaspoon Orange blossom or 1 teaspoon of vanilla essence or zest of a lemon finely chopped or all 3...

Preparation (the day before baking.)

Take the butter out of the refrigerator to soften or leave it out after breakfast it will need 1-2 hours room temperature to be the right texture or melt but leave to cool completely, also need time...

Put the eggs and sugar in a large bowl and whisk using an electric mixer until thick and pale—about 6-8 mins

Mix the flour and baking powder together then sift gradually, of the flour over the egg mixture fold it in using a spatula.

Add the flavouring of your choice now.

Pour or gradually add the butter into the batter mixture and gently fold them together until smooth, this can take a bit of time...

The dough must now rest—chill in a refrigerator for 3 hours at least but overnight is best {It's fine to leave it up to two days}.

To Bake

Basic Rule: Cold batter in a cold tray into a hot oven middle shelf.

1/2 hour before baking grease well with butter a 12-hole madeleine tray. Dust with flour – tapping out excess. Chill the tray in a freezer.

Preheat the oven to 220 degrees or 200 fan oven (gas 7)

Spoon the batter into the middle of moulds. (No need to spread it out)

Bake for 8-10 minutes. Watch out it can easily be less time depending on the oven and the size of madeleine tray. Mini madeleines take 5-7 minutes only.

Remove from the oven and immediately turn out on to a wire rack. Once cold add to your biscuit tin.

Your madeleine should be golden brown

CONCLUSION: The New Normal

The Vettas plus Juli's sister Stephanie and her husband Eric and their children Kirsten and Graham from Salt Lake City. Stephanie took this pic.

The last time all my family was able to be together was in July 2019.

Oh but I hate Covid. But there have been some good developments due to the pandemic. Zoom connecting us across the world is one of them. In November 2020, my family joined in the international online launch of the audio book of *Sculpting the Elephant* produced by Catherine O'Brien of Essential Audiobooks and recorded by the British-born Hollywood actor, Kamal Khan. I loved Kamal's recording. He perfectly captures my character of Gangabharti as Kamal sings Bollywood as well Hollywood, and he entertained us in song. Friends, family and readers from five continents enjoyed themselves together. It was 7.30 am in Los Angeles, 10:30 in New York and Montreal, 11.30 am in Chile and Newfoundland, 3.30 pm in the UK, 6.30 pm with Nancy in Kenya, and 9.30 pm in India where Sushma, who went with me on the Buddhist trail, spoke for our Indian family.

In 2010, an artist joined our family. Paul met Elizabeth Ludlow while at university, when she was doing a nursing degree. They were dating when Justin and Amita married and she came to the wedding. Not long after they drifted apart. When they met again they decided they didn't want to part. They each sold their properties and bought a 1930s house in Surrey, which was in need of a great deal of work. You'll understand by now that Vettas do renovation! The seven-year-old me couldn't have imagined that such upward mobility would be possible.

Once their new home was transformed, they organised a delightful wedding with a reception for ninety in their garden. Atam and I arranged to provide the catering and Elizabeth's parents stocked up with wine and champagne in France. Their garden looked magical after their friends finished decorating the marquee and hanging lanterns from the trees. Paul and Elizabeth gave us three delightful granddaughters quite quickly. Elizabeth balances parenthood, nursing and a growing career in art. The cover of *Sculpting the Elephant* incorporated an elephant drawn by Elizabeth. In the references, I have included samples of her work. You'll have gathered that, as well as for books, I have a passion for art so it's delightful having an artist in the family.

Adrian and Juli didn't make Paul and Elizabeth's wedding because they were rather busy. In Canada, my grandson, Tristan, was born on the wedding day!

∞

In 2001, the whole family headed to meet Juli's family in Newfoundland. It was a culture shock for me. It wouldn't be a sensible idea to get lost on a hike in Newfoundland—no one would ever find you! It's as big as England and Wales put together but has a population of approximately 500,000, of which half live in and around St Johns. The climate is harsh and the soil thin, so settlements survived against the odds. Maybe that is why the people are so nice: they have to support each other. As we drove towards Gros Morne to the accompaniment of the Beatles' Hey Jude, which Elysia and Amber loved, I joked that our four vehicles constituted a traffic jam.

Adrian and Juli live in Montreal, which is a French-speaking city, and Kerensa and Tristan attend French schools, so are bi-lingual. Compared with many families in 2021, ours is not particularly mixed. Despite that, we have family connections in India, Canada, the USA, a niece currently working in Uganda and some of Fopin's family in Mauritius. A nephew is working in Australia for three years where my brother Mike has many friends. That means we are directly connected to five continents. In today's UK, that is so normal that I fail to understand why little Englanders still exist and have such influence.

In 2021, we watched the Taliban take over again in Afghanistan and in Texas backwards-looking legislation banning abortion. Toxic fundamentalism seems to be on the march. At home, our government is hollowing out democratic norms and procedures in chilling pieces of legislation, after fostering continuous antipathy to foreigners, refugees and minorities who work hard to contribute to our society.

And yet.

I was riveted to the TV in September 2021 to watch eighteen-year-old Brit, Emma Raducanu, playing nineteen-year-old, Montreal-born,

Leylah Fernandez. Both of these young women of mixed ancestry were proud of their heritage and nationality, and played and spoke with determination and grace. This is the new normal. Diversity is healthy. In my opinion, it's not only healthy in a scientific sense but stimulates creativity and empathy.

Race, gender and class have shaped and constrained the opportunities and possibilities of my life. Atam and I have spent our lives creating a recipe from what was available to us. With food comes love and with love comes hope. I'm proud of my sons, their partners and my grandchildren. I hope they will see earth as the home we all share.

Here is my FINAL recipe: I sometimes abbreviate my granddaughter's names, Antonia, Alexandra and Anastasia to the 3As. Their recipe? Hot chocolate sprinkled with marshmallows, which is especially nice at the end of a long day and before settling down for the night.

Hot Chocolate with Marshmallows by the 3As

Put one dessert spoonful of drinking chocolate in a mug.
Stir in a little milk.
Top up with boiling water.
Sprinkle with marshmallows.

ENDNOTES

What began as an exercise in remembering became this memoir. I wanted the *Food of Love* to be about more than just me, and instead to reflect the changes in our society over the last seventy years. But would my friends and family be happy being a part of such a story published for anyone to read? I asked them and I want to thank them for their tolerance and support.

Special thanks to my grandchildren Elysia, Amber, Kerensa, Antonia, Tristan, Alexandra and Anastasia, who provided most of the delightful illustrations.

Thank you to Weimin He, who not only provided an illustration but also the caricature of me used on the back cover. The famous illustrator, Korky Paul, is a generous supporter of my village school and library, and provided the illustration for the library chapter. I first met the public artist Diana Bell at the launch of Oxford Castaways 2 in the Story Museum where my guests wrote in her giant book. She too sent a contribution. Thank you, Diana. And my daughter-in-law Elizabeth Vetta not only did an illustration for this book, but also the illustration for the cover of *Sculpting the Elephant*.

This is my third book for Claret Press. The talented book designer, Petya Tsankova, has worked on all three and *Food of Love* has been the most complicated. I love it. Thank you, Petya.

I'm honoured by the wonderful people who were prepared to read and endorse this book, as I have been honoured by so many in the past. If you are interested in them and some of the issues in my memoir please visit:

https://www.sylviavetta.co.uk/

My career as an author would not have been possible without the support of Claret Press. It's rare for a writer not to need an editor. I certainly needed one and found an exceptionally talented editor in Katie Isbester.

Thank you too to those of you who read this. What is the point of being a writer without readers? Ultimately it is you, the readers, who have made this all possible. My sincerest thanks.

References

Appetiser

The Hunting of the Shark: The Story Behind the Tale That Crash Landed on an Unsuspecting Oxford Suburban Street, Bill Heine, Oxfordfolio, 2011.
For more information, please see The Hunting of the Shark etc

Chapter 1: Flopsy 1952

The number of minutes parents spend with their children is dramatically higher now than it was in my childhood, rising from 50 minutes in 1965 to 150.
The Economist November 27, 2017

Chapter 3: Corsets, Rulers and Frozen Peas

Real GDP doubled between the early 1950s and the early 1970s.
https://www.theguardian.com/news/datablog/2009/nov/25/gdp-uk-1948-growth-economy

10% of grammar school students were working class.
Crowther Report of 1959, A Report of the Central Advisory Council of England

In 1945 the richest 0.01% of people in Britain had 123 times the mean national average of income. By 1965 it was halved to 62 times and by 1978 it was at its lowest at 28 times. By 2007, it had once again risen to 144 times and is rising still. "How Social Mobility Got Stuck," Danny Dorling, New Stateman, July 2013

Chapter 5: Faith Served Cold

In the fifties over 80% of the British population were Christian, and attended church or chapel either regularly or on special occasions. Most married in a church and had a Christian burial. In the last census barely 50% of population identified as Christian. **http://www.brin.ac.uk/**

Chapter 6: Smethwick 1963/4

Partition in India, including some of Atam's story **http://madrascourier.com/opinion/can-india-and-pakistan-overcome-partition/**

The Parliamentary Leper/ Colour and British Politics, Dr Dhani R Prem, Everest Press, 1965.

Chapter 7: Seretse Khama & the Parliamentary Leper

A Marriage of Inconvenience: The Persecution of Seretse and Ruth Khama, Michael Duffield, Unwin Press, 1990

Colour Bar: The Triumph of Seretse Khama and His Nation, Susan Williams, Penguin Press, 2016.

A United Kingdom, the film, 2016.

Chapter 8: Westminster

Thomas Dodson is the Collections & Digitisation Officer, for the Oxford Centre for Methodism and Church History, which corroborated my history of the college.

Chapter 14: Deeply Local and Sicily

In 1976, Simonetta invited us to spend a month in Sicily at their family estate set in ancient olive groves: an unforgettable experience. Simonetta's sister, Chiara, later converted the stable block and turned the Mose estate into a business so you can see the house on their website.
https://www.fattoriamose.com/

Chapter 16: Misogyny, CND and KADS

https://www.sylviavetta.co.uk/wp-content/uploads/2013/08/Victor_Glynn.pdf
Joe and Zara Shakespeare in Oxford Project **https://vimeo.com/123886243**

Greenham Common Protests **http://www.greenhamwpc.org.uk/**

Chapter 17: A Glass Ceiling and Scientific Racism

"The Cyril Burt Question: New Findings," D.D. Dorfman, *Science* Vol 201, No 4362, 29 September 1978.

Chapter 20: To the Jam Factory

A potted history of Jam Factory: **https://www.oxfordmail.co.uk/news/18881277.romanies-didnt-haggle-princess-margaret---antiques-memories-jam-factory/?**

Chapter 22: Beginnings and endings

The Oxford Times reported it because it involved a breach of the planning agreement for the golf course. Wellister Investments must have made an eye-watering profit in a short time.
https://www.oxfordmail.co.uk/news/6638731.golf-course-plan-blocked/

Chapter 23: An Opportunity that Changed My Life

Sylvia's feature on a TVADA event
https://www.oxfordmail.co.uk/news/2204195.next-trading-post-minutes-away-signed/

Amita's website: **www.lovethatjewellery.co.uk**

A few examples from over 1,000 review features by Sylvia
http://www.oxfordtimes.co.uk/news/1012466.The_portrait_of_the_artist_as_pure_genius/
http://www.oxfordtimes.co.uk/news/953952.An_empire_built_on_furniture/
http://www.swindonadvertiser.co.uk/news/11509882.Ai_Weiwei_show_has_a_stately_presence/
https://www.oxfordmail.co.uk/news/8958121.alfred-wallis-ben-nicholson-compton-verney/

Chapter 25: Everyone's Life is an Epic

The Changing Face of China, John Gittings, Oxford University Press, 2006

As our world becomes more integrated and we become more familiar with others' stories, the issue of cultural appropriation becomes ever more fraught, of which my experience with *Brushstrokes in Time* was a confusing and hurtful episode. British-Ghanaian scholar, Kwame Anthony Appiah and his Reith Lectures influenced my own thinking and I highly recommended listening to them for his clarity of thought, depth of learning and profound sensitivity.

The Reith Lectures: Mistaken Identities, Kwame Anthony Appiah (particularly 3 and 4, on Colour and Culture):

http://www.bbc.co.uk/programmes/b00729d9/episodes/player

Chapter 26: Oxtopia

Castaway lecture with images and film: **https://www.youtube.com/watch?v=6NvrzUnGE50**
Oxford Castaways, Oxford Castaways 2 and Oxford Castaways 3, Sylvia Vetta (Oxfordfolio). The features appeared in Oxfordshire Limited Edition from 2007 - 2016 .

http://madrascourier.com/biography/beyond-breaking-the-4-minute-mile-a-personal-tribute-to-sir-roger-bannister/

Chapter 27: Past is Future

Ashoka the Visionary: Life, Legend and Legacy, Ashok Khanna, Bloomsbury, India, 2020

Ashoka: the Search for India's Lost Emperor, Charles Allen, Abacus, 2013

Elizabeth Vetta (artist): **www.elizabethvetta.co.uk**

Chapter 28: Why Life is Not So Black and White

https://www.oxfordmail.co.uk/news/16956996.village-group-which-raised-500k-in-50-years-bows-out-with-last-ever-event/
https://bit.ly/3e3arNr OXMagazine interview with Nancy Muden-yo Hunt and Sylvia Vetta
https://www.oxfordmail.co.uk/news/18500465.read-black-lives-matter-protest-oxfordshire/
https://www.lovereading.co.uk/book/20163/Not-so-Black-and-White-by-Sylvia-Vetta-Nancy-Mudenyo-Hunt.html

Poems in an Exhibition for Standing Voice

http://www.oxfordmail.co.uk/news/15701324.Robin_Gibb__39_s_widow_reads_funeral_poem_to_raise_funds_for_charity/

Chapter 29: The Underestimated Importance of Libraries

Saving our libraries: the Pied Piper procession https://www.heraldseries.co.uk/news/8839325.Mitchell_besieged_by_angry_villagers/

An example of Atam Vetta's latest scientific interest: No Quantitative Trait Loci but welcome to new science of Gene Editing

This short paper traces the history of the rise of the polygenic hypothesis and its fall. It welcomes the advent of NEW science of "Gene Editing".

Research on polygenic traits, also known as Quantitative Traits by non-geneticists, was the craze of the 20th century; in particular, in the last quarter of it. Hundreds of papers on such traits were published starting with A R Jensen's notorious paper "How much can we boost IQ and scholastic achievement" in the *Harvard Educational Review* in 1969. In that paper Jensen argued that the status of black Americans cannot be improved because their genes were inferior. His followers in the USA were only concerned with the inferiority of black Americans. His followers in the UK were primarily concerned with the "poor" genes of the British working class. I too believed in polygenes and published a short paper "Evidence for polygenes" in the foremost scientific journal *NATURE* in 1976. Later in 1999, I published with my colleagues Capron and Duyme, (Capron et. al. 1999) a peer review paper, "Misconceptions of Biometrical IQists", in the journal *CPC*. That paper was commented on and criticised by thirteen European and US researchers and we replied. It took over a whole volume of that journal. In short, we all believed in the existence of polygenes. (A polygene is a gene with a very small effect and lots of polygenes are needed for a normally distributed genetic trait).

The concept of a polygenic trait with a normal distribution was the centre piece of A R Fisher's famous 1918 paper, "The correlation between relatives on the supposition of Mendelian inheritance". After WW2, Higher Education opportunities expanded vastly in the English speaking countries and Fisher's students became Professors of Genetics or Professors of Statistics in many English speaking universities.

Thus, his ideas and methods spread in the scientific community of the world. The name polygene was suggested by Professor Mathur of Birmingham University who was a student of Fisher.

Discarding the idea of polygenes:

The human genome was deciphered in the year 2000. It was found that there are only about 20K to 25K genes in the human genome. This was a far cry from over a million genes that we had expected. It was obvious that, given this small number, there was no room in the human genome for sets of polygenes, each set containing thousands of polygenes and giving rise to a polygenic trait. We were forced to discard the hypothesis of a human polygenic trait. Dr Plomin, a leading Jensen's type of researcher, claimed in a letter to the US journal *SCIENCE* that deciphering of the human genome proved that polygenes exist. I had to correct him in that journal that, on the contrary, it proves that there are no polygenes in the human genome. Later, other genomes were deciphered and no polygenes were discovered in any of them. It is, therefore, safe to conclude that Fisher's 1918 beautiful polygenic model will have to wait to be used when we discover a genome that has polygenes.

Most proponents of the polygenic hypothesis trace its origin to Jinks & Fulker (1970) and NOT to Fisher 1918 because they were Professor Jink's students. At that time Jinks, a student of Mathur who was a student of Fisher, was the Professor of Genetics at Birmingham University. At the same time Fulker was a Professor of Psychology at Birmingham. In 1970 there was no method of estimating Gene-Environment (GE) Interaction. In their 1970 paper Jinks and Fulker set about producing a formula for estimating GE interaction by considering a simple 2 gene model. In the rest of the paper, they analysed some available data assuming GE interaction= 0. The formula for GE interaction was their only original contribution. Professor Jinks' ex-students in the USA took the 1970 paper as their bible and published many papers based on it. In 1975, when reading for my PhD

Ph. D. at the Galton laboratory, UCL, I came across their paper. Being a mathematician, I had developed the habit of checking the mathematics of every paper I read. I found that in their simple 2 gene model, Jinks & Fulker had made a mistake and when that mistake is corrected their formula will always give GE interaction as 0. Thus, the formula was useless. My PhD supervisor communicated my correction to Professor Jinks and he invited us to his laboratory. In the presence of his students he accepted the mathematical error and asked us to send the correction to Herrnstein, the Editor of the *Psychological Bulletin* where the paper was published. Herrnstein declined to publish the correction but it soon became widely known. People in powerful positions rarely like facing the truth if it contradicts their agenda.

Gene Editing:

Regrettably, some non-geneticists are still publishing papers on QTL (Quantitative Trait Loci) i.e. the locus of a polygene. A recent example is a paper published by Kashyap in *Academia* relating to crops. It might, therefore, be of some use to explain to non-geneticists like him, the NEW science of gene editing and the manner in which it is likely to be used.

Gene editing enables a scientist to make changes in the DNA of an individual leading to a physical change in that individual. Thus, it is the science of altering the genetic material of a living organism by deleting a DNA sequence and inserting in its place a different DNA sequence. Its purpose is to improve some character of the individual. It can be used to remove a deformity, for example. In humans, gene editing can be used to correct a single point mutation such as Sickle Cell anaemia. Given time, gene editing will find greater uses.

Kashyap's *Academia* paper is mainly concerned with crops. It is, therefore, appropriate to report the experiment on gene editing of wheat that started on 18 October 2021 in the UK. 56,700 gene edited wheat seeds were planted in a field in North Hertfordshire, England. It is thought that the prevalent toasting of wheat and other cereal crops by breakfast-cereal manufacturers can make them carcinogenic (cancer causing). As this poses a (minor) cancer risk, a tight regulatory limit has been placed on the amount of toasting that cereal manufacturers are allowed to carry out – and they have complained that it makes their products taste "insipid". Now scientists are working on a new generation of cereal crop that have been gene-edited to make them far less likely to become carcinogenic. In this case, the technique has been used to reduce levels of the naturally occurring amino acid asparagine, which turns into the carcinogenic chemical acrylamide when wheat is processed into bread. That process increases substantially when the wheat or bread is toasted.

This is the first gene-editing trial since the government lifted its ban on gene edited crops in September 2021 and the first of a staple crop ever undertaken in Europe. Concerning this experiment, Professor Halford said "the tone of the plant breeders has changed completely" since the government lifted the ban. They are now thinking much more in terms of commercial development of gene edited crops rather than just research of the technology's potential – although it's still early days.

There is broad consensus among scientists that gene editing can play a key role in feeding a growing population as the climate changes. There are serious dangers if the gene editing falls in the hands of some "evil" people. There is also the danger that the technique could potentially upset the balance of nature in unforeseen ways, as a crop edited to be resistant to one disease, for example, may encourage another disease to flourish in its place. The morality of gene editing needs to be faced by scientists as well by governments. I am confident that we will use this new technique for the benefit of all humanity.

INDEX OF RECIPES

Starters, Snacks and Salads

Sylvia's Pakoras
Prawn Cocktail (sixties style)
Amita's Alloo Tikki Chaat
Pasta Fritta etc
Fopin's Mauritian Achard (Tumeric and Mustard preserved vegetables)
Helen Peacock's Kale Crisps

Main Course Dishes

Grandmother Elizabeth's Cornish Pasties
Doris Harry's Fish with mashed potatoes and parsley sauce
Atam's Cauliflower Curry
Amita's Daal
Icolyn Smith's Jamaican Jerk Chicken
Justin's Moussaka

Judy Kay Bard's Chilli, American Style
Rama's Saag (spinach) with Makki Roti
Partap and Sneh Chopra's 'Moonlight' Matter Paneer (Peas Paneer)
Paul's Black Bean Burrito
Caroline and Leilei Qu's Easy Peasy Pepper Chicken
Margaret Newton's Ragout with Apricots
MINUTAL EX PRAECOQUIS from the Ancient Roman recipe book by
APICIUS

Cakes and Desserts

Doris Harry's Scones
Gill Hedge's Danish Girl with a Veil
Simonetta Agnello Hornby's Almond Cake without flour
Dominique Henderson's Madeleines
Elysia and Amber Vetta's Chocolate Brownies

Good Night

Hot chocolate with Marshmallows (Antonia, Alexandra and Anastasia Vetta)

Claret Press shares engaging stories about the real issues of our changing world. Since it was founded in 2015, Claret Press has seen its titles translated into German, shortlisted for a Royal Society of Literature award, sold on to larger publishers and climb the bestseller list. Each book probes the entanglement of the political, the historical and the everyday—but always with the goal of creating an engaging read.

If you enjoyed this book, then we're sure you'll find more great reads in the Claret Press library. Sylvia Vetta's two books with Claret Press are *Brushstrokes in Time* and *Sculpting the Elephant*.

Subscribe to our mailing list at **www.claretpress.com** to get news of our latest releases, bespoke zoom events and the occasional adorable photo of the Claret Press pets.

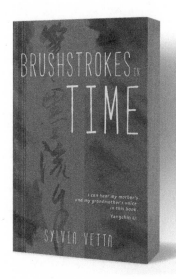

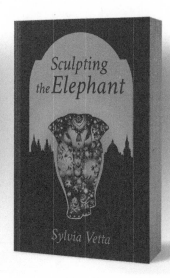